✦

For Sam

✦

Scott Craig's

The Story
Next Door

For information, please contact Pleasant City Press, LLC, at Post Office Box 562, Suttons Bay, Michigan 49682, or pleasantcitypress@yahoo.com.

Printed and bound in the United States.
First printing 2013.

ISBN 978-0-9793596-6-8

CIP 2012919912

Cover and book design by Saxon Design Inc.

Scott Craig's
The Story Next Door

PLEASANT CITY PRESS

www.pleasantcitypress.com

✦

If history were taught in the form of
stories, it would never be forgotten.

RUDYARD KIPLING

✦

Contents

Foreword by Ed Spray   xi

Introduction   xv

Doers   1

Peg Simmons   3

Larry Glass   7

Piper Goldson   11

Matt Myers   15

Linda Lindquist   19

Jim Kareck   23

Bea Kimmerly   27

Norm Wheeler   31

Rebecca Lessard   35

Janet Weiler   39

Lisa Wehr   43

Lud Ashley   47

Dreamers   51

Sharon Sutterfield   53

Mike Grosvenor   55

John Scott   59

Bill Livingston   63

Heroes   67

Bob Maynard   69

Jerry Linenger   73

Bob Willard   77

Dick Grout   81

Ted Lanham   85

Fred Atkinson   89

Foodies 93

John and Phyllis Kilcherman 95

Bernie Rink 99

Bill Fraser 103

John and Julia Brabenec 107

John and Anne Hoyt 111

Jess Piskor and Abra Berens 115

Pram and Suzanne Acharya 119

Larry Mawby 123

Artists 127

Bill Hosner 129

Jim and Gail Leone 133

Fred Petroskey 137

Guido Goldkuhle 141

Bob James 145

Dave Lint 149

Lynne Rae Perkins 153

Fighters 157

Sandy Blumenfeld 159

Martha Baker 163

Keith Burnham 167

Bill Irvine 171

Bob Stehouwer 175

Stefani Pentiuk 179

Afterword 185

Acknowledgments 187

About the Author 189

Foreword

I first met Scott Craig in the summer of 1966. Scott was a high-profile producer-director for NBC Chicago. I was a summer-relief TV stage manager. Scott was in the early stages of a remarkably successful career making television documentaries; I was a fresh out-of-college television neophyte looking for a role model. In Scott I found what I was looking for. Little did I know how our careers would intertwine so tightly, and a life-long friendship ensue.

Chicago at the time was in the midst of a tremendously creative period, energized by brilliant writers, critics and unstoppable social activists. Among them were the renowned newspaper columnist Mike Royko and the legendary oral historian of common Americans, Studs Terkel. Both would later be awarded Pulitzer Prizes for their writing. Both were good friends of Scott Craig. He would eventually produce award-winning documentaries about each man. I think

Scott Craig (front, far right), mid-1970's with an NBC crew, Chicago

Scott Craig with a CBS crew on location, Chicago 1981

some of the influence of Royko and Terkel rubbed off on Scott as did the richness of life in the great melting pot of Chicago.

In 1975 Scott and I teamed up and joined CBS Chicago. Scott continued to create documentaries and I became Program Director. We worked together in these capacities for another decade. Year after year Scott's documentaries and specials would win just about every national and local media award given. Many wondered at his success and tried to guess his secret. I, of course, had learned that secret years earlier. Simply put, Scott is at heart a consummate storyteller—in the best definition of the word. He has a unique ability to tell human stories in real and human terms.

I eventually moved on to take a management position with CBS in Los Angeles. Scott remained in Chicago. He continued to make programs about that city, but increasingly he was sought out to deal with broader subjects for national audiences. In 1994, when I was asked to start HGTV, the Home and Garden Television Network, I knew it was absolutely vital to find skilled producers. Most importantly, I needed storytellers to bring warmth and human interest to a network about "things." I immediately turned to Scott

Scott Craig's The Story Next Door

Craig. For six years he produced two series for HGTV, "Extreme Homes" and "The Good Life." Both were especially well-received by our audiences. And there was a good reason: They were filled with amazing, heart-warming tales of ordinary people living extraordinary lives.

When Scott retired, I knew he couldn't sit in a rocker on his porch, but I had no idea he would create a new radio series. I should have guessed he'd continue spinning stories. And what stories they are! I am delighted he has compiled many of these tales in this book so that we all can have them at hand to enjoy at any time. As you read them, I know they'll cause a smile, a belly laugh or even a lump in the throat. That's what a great storyteller brings to the game.

Ed Spray
Co-founder, HGTV
President, Scripps Networks Interactive (retired)

Scott Craig, late 1980's, directing Hal Holbrook, Los Angeles

Introduction

This project began in 2006. I had recently retired from a forty-five year career as a television producer-director and was looking for something new to do. I had been an avid listener of Interlochen Public Radio since its inception. I decided to seek a meeting with the station manager, Thom Paulson. That was arranged and I volunteered to do some announcing, perhaps reading copy about program underwriters. Paulson said that would be fine but instead why didn't I take some time to develop an idea … maybe something creative that I could give to the station.

On the drive back to my home in Leland, I came up with a concept. As a professional documentary producer, I had prided myself on being pretty good at handling human-interest. Also, largely because of the experiences I had during my career, I discovered that everybody, and I mean everybody, has a story worth hearing. Perhaps I could create a radio series based on the premise of telling stories about ordinary people. On that drive home I even thought of a title, "The Story Next Door." To date, Interlochen Public Radio has broadcast more than fifty of them.

The original idea was simply to present my tales on the radio and that, of course, is what I have done. But broadcasts disappear into the ether. As time passed, I began to think these stories could be shared in a more permanent way. The result is this book.

Some of the punctuation and sentence structure in these profiles reflect that they were written to be presented orally. In fact, to enjoy them as originally intended, you too may wish to read them aloud.

Since the time of their original airing, some of the stories have changed. Lives have moved on. Some of the featured people have left this world. However, I have decided not to update. You will read about these folks in the same way that I originally told their stories on the air.

Scott Craig
April 2013

Doers

One of my best moves is to surround
myself with friends who instead of asking,
"Why?" are quick to ask "Why not?"
That attitude is contagious.

Oprah Winfrey

Life is a gamble at terrible odds.
If it was a bet,
you wouldn't take it.

Tom Stoppard

I've always made a total effort,
even when the odds are against me.
I never quit trying.
I never felt that I didn't have
a chance to win.

Arnold Palmer

You only live once, but if you do it right,
once is enough.

Mae West

Peg Simmons

MARCH 2011

When I called her to ask if we could get together she said, "You know, I'm one hundred-and-a-half years old!" Then she gave me directions.

Her home is in a wooded subdivision called Settlers Cove on the western edge of Traverse City near Interlochen. Peg Simmons turned out to be a short, trim woman. Even though she was using a walker, her stature was ramrod straight. Her eyes sparkled from behind her spectacles.

I wondered what I was going to ask a hundred-and-a-half year-old woman, but I needn't have worried. She led the way. "You know, it's twenty-one below in Fairbanks this morning," she said. I asked how she knew that. "Oh," she replied, "I check it every day on the Weather Channel. I lived in Alaska in the '40's. Please sit down."

"When did you start counting half-year birthdays?" I asked. "I don't," she answered. "Others do it for me."

"Do you live alone?"

"Yes. I don't want to go into assisted living. I have too much to do."

I learned that in early childhood, Peg had been raised by her single mother and her grandparents. They owned a resort, a grocery store, a restaurant, and a bar near Bay City. Their properties were adjacent to an amusement park with rides and a nice beach. Customers came on the Interurban Trolley from Bay City, bringing blankets and picnic lunches to spend the day. The park also had a summer theatre where barnstorming vaudevillians performed. Stars like the Marx Brothers, Marie Dressler, and Will Rogers stayed at her grandfather's resort and Peg rubbed shoulders with them. "Oh, that W.C. Fields," she moaned. "He was a piece of work!"

When Peg was twelve, her mother remarried. Her new husband owned one of the rides at the park. Soon thereafter, Peg began selling tickets and running the Ferris wheel. "There was nothing to it," she told me.

At fourteen, her stepfather taught her how to drive the family's seven-passenger Hudson touring car. He also made her familiar with everything under the hood, as well as how to jack up the car and change a tire. "I drove for eighty-five years. I just quit last year. I never had a ticket or an accident," she told me with pride.

I asked her what she could recall about Prohibition. She said her grandfather closed his bar but didn't get rid of the liquor. He didn't sell it, but cronies would stop by occasionally on their way home from work and imbibe. One of the wives didn't like the condition in which her hubby came home, so she turned Grandpa in to the sheriff who reluctantly jailed him. The next day Peg's grandmother went to visit him but the sheriff turned her away, saying, "You can't see him now." She came back on subsequent days and got the same answer. She finally asked what was going on. The sheriff had to admit that her husband wasn't there. It seems the sheriff was letting Grandpa out of jail every afternoon to go to the movies. He was freed within a week.

Did Peg attend a university? "Yes," she answered. "I went to the Old Cow College. That's what we called Michigan State back then." The crash of '29 ended school for her. Luckily she got a job with Western Union making seventeen cents an hour. She became skilled in Morse Code and then in wireless communication.

When World War II broke out Peg joined the Civilian Army (the WACs didn't exist yet) and was sent to Alaska where she served for three years as a communications expert. There, at a nightclub, she met a soldier named Gordon Simmons. After three weeks of dating they decided to marry at war's end ... and that's what they did.

They moved to New Jersey where Gordon went to work for GE in the International Division. During his career he received assignments to such places as Spain, Peru, Mexico, Argentina, and

Brazil. Over the years the couple often visited Peg's folks in Michigan and Gordon fell in love with the state. So in 1984, when he retired, they moved to Traverse City.

Gordon died just short of his ninetieth birthday. Peg has kept busy doing a lot of volunteer work. A friend recently gave her a typewriter so she could write her memoirs. "I really have had a good life," she told me.

As I was leaving, I asked her about W.C. Fields. He has always intrigued me. "Well, I was just a small girl," she replied, "but I can tell you from first-hand experience, he really *did not* like little children."

Peg Simmons … one-of-a-kind at one hundred-and-a-half years of age. ⚹

Larry Glass

JUNE 2007

He's a big man with a brush cut. His face can alternate from a no-nonsense frown to a sly grin at the drop of a hat.

He went to Miami University in Ohio on an athletic scholarship. There he was a standout on both the baseball and basketball teams. After his junior year he signed a contract with the Cleveland Indians as a pitcher. Unfortunately, he hurt his arm in the minor leagues and his professional career ended quickly. The good news was that the Indians had given him a $4,000 signing bonus. It was enough to allow him to marry his college sweetheart, Dee, in the fall of 1956.

He went back to Miami, finished his degree, and set out to seek a career as a high school English teacher and coach. During an interview with one school's athletic director, he was asked about his goal in life. Without hesitation Larry replied, "I want to be a Big Ten basketball coach." The AD tried not to laugh.

Larry's high school teams did relatively well. One day, to his surprise, he got a call from Northwestern University in Evanston, Illinois. Old friends from Miami were on the athletic faculty there and had recommended him for the position of freshman basketball coach. He took the job, advanced within the department, and in 1963 Larry Glass was named head basketball coach at Northwestern. He'd done it! At just twenty-eight years of age, he had achieved what he thought was his life's goal.

But it turned out to be a tough job. Northwestern, the only private school in the Big Ten, has very high academic standards which meant Larry could only recruit very smart kids. The competition did not have the same requirement. In addition, Northwestern has high ethical standards. There could be no recruiting "hanky panky." Larry adhered to that but watched helplessly as some of his opponents continually broke the rules. It wore on him and in his sixth year, he felt he simply couldn't continue to compete on a field that was so badly slanted against him. So in 1969, at the age of thirty-four, feeling burned out, he resigned from his dream job.

Now, what was he going to do with his life? He and Dee had four children! Somehow they hit on the idea of owning a resort somewhere, a place with some cabins on a lake. With that and a job in a local high school, he felt they could get by. The young couple set out on that quest, looking at thirty-two different sites.

On a trip to northern Michigan, they came across a resort for sale just south of Leland on Lake Leelanau. It seemed to fit the bill. They bought it, named it the Glass House and moved in.

No position was open at nearby schools so Larry took work as the night auditor at the Sugar Loaf Ski Resort. A year later, he landed a job teaching English at the Leland High School.

At about the same time, basketball teams for girls were being formed in the area. Larry's second daughter, Laurie, was entering high school and wanted to compete. She went to Leland's Athletic Director with a list of seven girls who also wanted to play. A local woman coached the team for the first two years.

In 1977, Laurie was a junior and her sister Rebecca was a freshman. The girls approached their dad and begged him to be their coach. "Who wants to coach girls?" Larry thought to himself. But his daughters persisted and he finally relented.

That year they won 13 games and lost 5. The next year they were 18 and 3. The next …19 and 2. Then the Leland girls blew the roof off. In 1980, they won 27 games, lost none, and won the Class D State Championship. They did it again in 1981, and again in 1982. Three state basketball championships in three years! Young women from Larry's teams received scholarships from the likes of Michigan, Dartmouth, Michigan State, and Northwestern.

Larry retired from coaching but kept on teaching English. Eventually they sold the resort and in 1994 he retired completely. And that should be the end of this tale, with Larry just taking it easy. But there's more to his story.

In the year 2000, Larry was sixty-five. He had a granddaughter who was now a junior at Leland. Another was a freshman. A third granddaughter, named Alisha, was in the eighth grade. All were playing basketball. When he learned that the girls coaching job was opening up again, it gave him pause. He could sit back and just watch his granddaughters play, or, heaven forbid, he could come out of retirement.

I'm sure you can guess what he did. That's right. He coached the Leland girls for six more years. They didn't reach the dizzying heights of his 1980's teams but they did pretty well, regularly winning district and regional championships.

So now, that's the end of the story. Right? Well, not quite. You may remember I mentioned Larry's granddaughter Alisha. She was a good basketball player but she was even better at another sport: volleyball.

It turns out that Larry's daughter Laurie (Alisha's mother) had taken over the girls' volleyball program at Leland. Her teams dominated the league and won the Class D State Championship. Then, with Alisha starring, they did it again! The Glass legacy continued. In the year 2006, Alisha was named Michigan's Gatorade Player of the Year, Miss Volleyball for the State of Michigan, and Michigan Female Athlete of the Year (for all sports in schools of all sizes.) What's more, she received a full scholarship to Penn State University.

As for Larry, he has once again retired. There are three more granddaughters who will soon be going to Leland High School, but he says, "No more coaching. Enough is enough." We'll see.

Upon reflection, Larry realizes that he once thought he'd achieved his greatest dream when at twenty-eight he became a Big Ten coach, only to discover far greater satisfaction and happiness at a small high school in a little town on a rural peninsula in northern Michigan. When asked to name his proudest accomplishment, he answered quickly, "I've got four great children. It's wonderful to really, really like your own kids. That's better than all the other stuff." ♣

Piper Goldson

MAY 2007

Most days you'll find her surrounded by great art in the Suttons Bay gallery that she has owned for eighteen years. She's an attractive, dark-haired, regal-looking woman, and at a glance you can tell she's a lady with impeccable taste. Don't let that put you off though. She's an incredibly open person with a ready laugh.

Piper is a graduate of Northwestern University with a major in literature and art history. She had a fine career in Chicago beginning as a free-lance journalist. She then went to work for a highly regarded architect as a kind of business manager. You see, while the architect was a gifted designer and artist, he was terrible about mundane things like paying bills. Piper filled that gap in his business and kept the wolf from the door. Mostly. One day in 1981, she got a call from the president of a bank. His name was Harry. He was calling because the architect was behind on a loan. Piper assured Harry that all would be well. They talked a bit longer and as the conversation progressed they both felt a connection. Plans were made to get together. They met for lunch about a week later and found that conversation was easy. They also discovered that both had a love for classical music.

Piper asked what he had done before banking and a fascinating tale emerged. It seems that Harry had grown up in Chicago and attended Austin High School, the cradle of an astonishing array of jazz musicians, including Benny Goodman. Harry followed in the tradition taking up the clarinet. He became accomplished with the instrument and soon was landing gigs with Big Bands in and around Chicago. When the bands began to tour, Harry went with them, dropping out of high school. He traveled the country with the likes of Claude Thornhill.

When the Korean War broke out, a recruiter told Harry that if he joined up he could be a member of the Fifth Army Band. He enlisted, only to discover that he'd been assigned to a position in Army Intelligence. He put his clarinet aside.

When the war ended, Harry returned to Chicago to find the Big Band Era in decline. So, he gathered up his instruments and sold them. He got his GED, went to college, and eventually ended up with a graduate degree in banking from Rutgers University. What followed was a highly successful career with financial institutions in California, New York, and Chicago.

Piper asked him if he could still play the clarinet. "Oh, I don't know," answered Harry. "I haven't picked one up in years."

The lunch ended with warm feelings. Piper and Harry began to see each other regularly. She discovered that he was going to have a birthday soon. She had a friend who was in the woodwind business. She went to see him, bought a clarinet, and presented it to Harry on his birthday. He was touched. He picked it up and began to play.

The music poured effortlessly from his instrument.

It was like he was a kid again playing with the Big Bands.

It was as if he'd never put it down.

Piper was thrilled … and moved.

She and Harry began to play duets. (Piper is an accomplished pianist.) They performed classical music for their own amusement.

Four months after their first date, Piper and Harry Goldson were married. That was twenty-six years ago.

One day in 1986, they took a short vacation trip to Traverse City, a location that Harry had visited as a child and remembered fondly. The North Country experience enchanted them and they began to look for a place to buy, finding what they were looking for in Suttons Bay. At first they used it occasionally on weekends and holidays, but then Harry realized he could do his banking and investment business from anywhere, so they moved north permanently. Harry encouraged Piper to open the art gallery.

On the side, Harry began to play his clarinet with a group of Traverse City musicians. They did it for fun in their spare time playing mostly classical fare, then transitioning to jazz. They made their first public appearance in 1993. In that same year, Harry produced his first album, recording it in Traverse City. It was well received. Encouraged, Harry contacted some West Coast connections and made a second recording in Los Angeles with some nationally known musicians. Again, the CD sold nicely.

That winter, Jim Milliman, the owner of Hattie's Restaurant in Suttons Bay, sought out Harry and Piper. He had been so impressed by Harry's playing that Jim suggested he do something on a grand scale in the summer time, perhaps a venue that included other musicians under a tent in Suttons Bay. His idea resonated with the Goldsons.

In 1993, the Suttons Bay Jazz Festival took root. This summer will be its fifteenth year. Piper and Harry are listed as founders — and that's true, but Piper runs the show. Of course, Harry has always been a featured performer but guest stars have included Ramsey Lewis, Ahmad Jamal, Marion McPartland and Bob James. The audiences have been large and enthusiastic.

In recent years, Harry's interests in banking have diminished as his musical popularity has grown. In the last fourteen years, he has recorded nine albums that have found audiences all over the world. Reviews of his work have been glowing and sales brisk.

And so, let's return to that birthday present, Piper's gift to Harry of a clarinet. It was a thoughtful gift that awakened a talent that had been dormant for thirty years … a gift that has brought pleasure and joy to thousands of people … and happiness to a former banker and to Piper, who is the love of his life. ⋏

Matt Myers

DECEMBER 2011

We were sitting in a coffee shop on Front Street in Traverse City. I asked my guest across the table about his growing-up years. "You really want to know?" he asked. "When my brother and I were little, our father was in prison."

That got my attention!

His name is Matt Myers. He's thirty-two years old — tall, lean, and muscular, with long dark hair pulled back in a ponytail. His eyes have an intense look that let you know he is a good listener.

He continued his story. His brother, Keegan, is two years younger. Early in their lives their family lived well, very well. They had a waterfront home on a point on the Old Mission Peninsula. There were cars, boats, an airplane, and a second home in Aspen, Colorado where the family spent half of each year. Then one day, the authorities swooped in and arrested Matt's dad. For a number of years, it turned out, he'd been a major figure in a large marijuana operation.

It was 1985, the year most everything came crashing down for the Myers family. Dad was locked up in prison. The cars and boats were hauled away. Gone were the plane and the house in Colorado. Income dried up and investments were taken. The only thing they were allowed to keep was the home on Old Mission. The boys' mother held the family together and eked out a living.

The brothers found themselves fairly isolated; not many playmates lived nearby. As a result they grew closer together. The beach and the bay were their playground. They heard about kiteboarding and decided to give it a try, teaching each other how to do it.

For those of you who don't know, kiteboarding is pretty much what it sounds like. A rider, using a surfboard, hangs onto a control bar attached to a large kite. It's exhilarating, but it's considered an "extreme sport," and if you're not careful, the result can be very serious. Here in our North Country, riders wait for high winds howling across Lake Michigan in the early spring and late fall. They don wet suits, head out into the gale, and fly from wave to wave at high speeds.

As the brothers worked at gaining kiteboarding skills, they learned a lot about nature — how to understand the wind, the water, and the weather. They also learned that they needed to rely on each other, and a deep bond was formed.

After six years, their father was released from prison. Matt was twelve. Keegan was ten. He took a job with Traverse City's legendary Father Fred and was involved with the formation of the priest's wonderful foundation that serves the needy. I said to Matt, "That was quite a change for your dad." Matt looked me straight in the eye. "No," he answered. "It wasn't a change. He was a good man when he went to prison and he was a good man when he came out. He had just done the wrong thing."

Matt and his brother attended Michigan State University. They worked their way through school and both graduated with near-perfect four-point grade averages.

Next they travelled, kiteboarding wherever the big winds blew … Tahiti, Argentina, Bora Bora. Everywhere they visited they'd say, "You know, this is really nice, but northern Michigan is better."

In time they returned to Traverse City, opened a small shop, and taught kiteboarding. It was fun, but pretty much of a hand-to-mouth operation. They discovered that the best boarding places were to be found all along state highway M22, a beautiful winding road that follows the Lake Michigan shore through Manistee and Benzie Counties and encircles all of the Leelanau Peninsula. In all of their travel, they had never encountered such a spectacular stretch of land and fresh water along a single highway. And it was from that realization that they focused on the road's sign … that black square with the white diamond inside imprinted with the black letters "M22." They turned the sign into a logo and made a few sample T-shirts that they gave to friends who loved them. So in 2005, the brothers began making T-shirts and stickers in earnest. The next year they opened a shop on Front Street. It was an immediate hit.

Today, their store overflows with cups, glasses, flags, bumper stickers, road signs, sweatshirts, sweatpants, hoodies, caps, water bottles and, of course, T-shirts … all emblazoned with the bold M22 logo. Sales are booming. Expansion is in the works. In northern Michigan, their products are seen and sold everywhere. They are so popular that the brothers have acquired a series of trademarks to discourage copycats.

Matt says, "The key to our business is that it's fun. We wouldn't do it if it weren't fun. It's growing… and so are we."

And there you are. Two brothers who survived a rocky childhood and have found a nice niche, one that still gives them lots of time for kiteboarding.

I asked Matt, if he had learned anything from all of this. His eyes narrowed and I felt he was thinking of his father when he answered. "I've learned you really can do what you want to do. Just pick the right thing."

Matt Myers appears to have done just that. ⚓

Linda Lindquist

March 2007

Linda Lindquist is an attractive young woman with long blond hair and the erect stature of an athlete. Northern Michigan has been a part of her life for as long as she can remember. That's because her father came here as a child, summering in Leland at the family cottage. Her mother did the same, but her family's place was on North Manitou Island.

During the wintertime, Linda and her family lived in the western suburbs of Chicago.

Linda learned to sail on Lake Leelanau. She loved the sport and became very good at it. So good, that now as an adult, she is quite active in Big Boat racing all over the world. She's even participated in the America's Cup. Today she wears a gorgeous Rolex wrist watch which she received as a prize when she and her sailing team won a world championship last year. That's an exciting story, but not the one I want to tell about Linda.

Let's start with the fact that Linda was beautiful and successful, but she had not been terribly lucky in the romance department. Put simply, she had not found the love of her life. She was living in New York City and working in the publishing business. About eight years ago, she felt she needed to get a fresh start, so she moved back to the Midwest, to Chicago, and a new job with a firm that specializes in executive coaching and leadership development. She liked the idea of being in Chicago again because it was closer to northern Michigan. It meant she'd be able to spend more weekends on Lake Leelanau.

One day, while at work, she received a call on her cell phone from a friend in San Francisco. She walked out on the balcony for a little more privacy than her office afforded. The balcony overlooked Michigan Avenue and the most upscale neighborhood in downtown Chicago. Lake Michigan sparkled nearby. As she talked with her friend, Linda heard a tremendous roar and looked up to see six sleek jet fighters flying by in close formation. They were so noisy she had to pause in her phone conversation. She explained to her friend that the Chicago Air and Water show was scheduled for the upcoming weekend and that the jets were apparently practicing for it.

"What color are the planes?" her friend asked.

"Red, white, and blue," Linda replied.

"Oh," said her friend, "those are the Thunderbirds, the Air Force precision flying team. If they come by again, wave at the lead plane. The pilot is a friend of mine. He's a really neat guy."

So as luck would have it, the Thunderbirds did come back making an identical pass. Linda, standing on the balcony, waved at the lead plane as she had been instructed.

Still on the phone, her friend said, "His name is Brian Bishop and his email address is …" and she spelled it out.

Back at her desk, Linda thought, "What the heck!" and she emailed Brian saying, "I was the blond on the balcony overlooking Michigan Avenue waving at you. We have a mutual friend in San Francisco." Linda mentioned her name and continued, "If you'd like to get together for a drink or a sail on Lake Michigan, let me know."

When Brian received the email, he immediately telephoned the San Francisco friend and asked, "Who is this Linda Lindquist?" Apparently, the answer pleased him because the next night Linda and Brian, a dashing Air Force commander, met at Chicago's Navy Pier. One thing led to another and, a year and a half later, they married. That was June of 2001.

Brian continued to fly as the lead commander of the Thunderbirds for two more years. Then he was promoted to piloting F16s, and served as wing commander on an Air Force base in South Korea. More recently, he has been assigned to a position in the Pentagon. Not long ago, Linda and Brian bought their own beautiful cottage on Lake Leelanau and spend "leave time" there happily together whenever they can.

Linda Lindquist-Bishop ... a young woman who dared to wave at a low-flying jet ... and started a wonderful new chapter in her life. ⚘

Jim Kareck

DECEMBER 2006

Jim Kareck is a stocky fellow with a voice that can knock out a wall when he chooses to use it that way. He says he's in his early seventies, but he looks much younger. He's retired now and lives in a home south of Leland that overlooks Lake Leelanau. Just to keep active in the summertime, he works a few days a week as a tournament manager in the pro shop of a golf club. One of his duties is to organize the weekly Men's Day event. Every Wednesday, at eight in the morning, forty or so golfers gather near the flagpole to find out what the format of the week's game will be. Jim announces it using that big voice of his so that all the men, including the deaf ones, will get the message. Where did he develop his vocal strength? Well, that's an important part of his story.

Jim grew up on a fifty-acre farm near Grand Rapids. A farm of that size could barely support his family. He went to school in Grand Rapids and played football. He was named to the All City Team in his senior year. Jim was a good student but had no hope of going on for a college education. His family simply didn't have the means to send him. Therefore, Jim had taken some shop classes in high school, assuming that he would become a tool and die maker.

Soon after graduation in 1950, a couple of buddies called and tried to talk Jim into enrolling at Grand Rapids Junior College. "We can all play football together there," they pleaded. Jim thanked them but said his folks just didn't have the where-with-all for him to even think about attending college.

Apparently, Jim's father overheard the conversation and it set him to thinking. After a couple of days, he took his son out on the farm and pointed out a two-acre plot of ground. It was low-lying and still soggy from the spring rains. "When that dries out," his father said, "let's plant it with sweet corn. Then we'll sell it and see if we can come up with some money so that maybe you can go to that college." And a couple of weeks later, when the land was ready, that's exactly what they did. Working together, they put in the seeds for the sweet corn.

It was early September before the corn matured. Jim and his dad picked it and filled an open farm trailer. The next morning at four, they were set up at the Farmer's Market in Grand Rapids. They put up a sign that read "SWEET CORN – 25¢ A DOZEN." "You stay here," his father said, "and I'll go look around to see who is selling what and for how much." Jim remained with the trailer and did pretty well. In fact, he had sold half the load by the time his father returned. "Nobody else has any sweet corn," his dad reported excitedly. "Because we planted later than the others, we're IT! Raise the price to fifty cents a dozen!"

Jim hastily crayoned a new sign and, lo and behold, a man walked up and bought the rest of the load. All of it! Jim and his father had sold out and were back home by six-thirty in the morning. They counted the money. They had made almost two hundred dollars! It was enough for tuition and books. He quickly enrolled at the Grand Rapids Junior College.

Jim got good grades there and was a starter on the football team for two years. In the summers he worked on the farm earning just enough to stay in school.

In 1952, he got a call from Albion College, offering a scholarship, based on his good academic record. Of course, it didn't hurt that he was a good football player as well. Again at Albion, he achieved in class, majoring in physical education. He played on an undefeated football team there. Jim decided he'd like to be a teacher and a coach. Upon graduation, he was hired by Albion High School where, at first, he coached football and track. Then he started a swimming program at the school. After eight years, he accepted a position at Flint Central High School where he coached swimming and golf. He also taught physical education, biology, and physiology. He did that for the next twenty-seven years.

Flint Central was a tough city school. There were not a lot of experienced golfers and swimmers within the student body. Jim developed systems for identifying kids with potential. For example, early each fall he gave all the new boys a swimming test. He'd pick out the better ones and recruit them for the team. "My greatest thrill," he says, "was taking a rookie and turning him into a champion."

His teams did pretty well over the years, but there was more to it than that. The young swimmers Jim coached learned the joy of being a part of a team, the value of hard work, the thrill of winning, and the character to stand proud even in defeat. His golfers learned the fun of the game, sportsmanship, honor, strategy, and the practical application of some math. A few went on to become golf professionals.

Jim is just as proud of the young people he had in his academic classes. Like all teachers, he thrills when he hears of the achievements of former students. One, who stays in touch, called the other day just to check in. He's the guy who developed the satellite guidance system for automobiles.

Today, when I hear Jim bellowing instructions to forty golfers at Men's Day, I understand he developed that big voice over the years getting the attention of twenty-four unruly boys in a swimming pool. And by now, I'm sure you also understand that Jim touched and influenced hundreds and hundreds of young lives. It all was made possible because of a two-acre patch of sweet corn and a father who looked for a way to give his son a chance for a college education. ⚜

Bea Kimmerly

December 2009

I had been told she was someone I should meet because she was an "older" lady with a real spark about her. I discovered she lives at the end of a long, leafy country lane on a hill just south of Omena. The house is a neat, white clapboard place built in the late 1920's. It's surrounded by a wide, well-cared for lawn and thick woods. Her car was sitting in the drive when I arrived, a rather sporty model.

Inside, her house was immaculate. I met her in the living room, a white-haired woman who seems to get around pretty well. I discovered there's a pleasant aura about her. I learned that she lives alone, cooks for herself, loves to read, and has good friends. She had driven to Suttons Bay and back that morning to visit some of them. She told me that not long ago she had made trips to Germany and Spain, and more recently to Costa Rica. No question about it, Bea Kimmerly is healthy, active, and full of life. It did surprise me though when I learned her age. She's ninety-seven!

I did some quick math. She was born in 1912. That was only forty-seven years after Lincoln was assassinated. Later, I did a little searching and discovered that when she was born, women could not vote in this country. In the year of her birth, Woodrow Wilson became president and the Titanic sank. I was in the presence of someone who put the history of our country in some perspective. I realized once more that America has a very short history … and Bea Kimmerly has seen much of it.

She grew up in downstate Alma. As a college kid, she spent a summer waiting tables at the Cedar Lodge on Northport Point. There she met and fell in love with Myles Kimmerly who also worked at the Point. They married and settled in Northport where Myles worked at a general store. In the Depression, Myles was lucky to keep his job and they survived on fifteen dollars a week. Yet, Bea remembers those years fondly. "Of course, we had no money," she said, "but nobody did." There were potluck suppers, cards, and music. People talked a lot, laughed, and played simple games. "We gardened, we canned, and we got along. Those were good times for just being folks and enjoying each other." She remembers when they got their first radio, a Philco. "It cost almost a week's pay," she laughingly told me. It surprises her to observe how many things people think they need now to be happy and it saddens her to see folks glued to their computers and cell phones.

As the years passed, Bea and Myles had three children. Their oldest son died of cancer at age eighteen. For a long time, they ran the general store in Omena. During that period, Myles was appointed Justice of the Peace. Bea says it was not unusual for police to bring in a culprit during working hours, which meant Myles had to retire to the back of the establishment to hold court.

Everybody in the family put in time at the store. Their patrons were locals, migrant workers, Native Americans, and resorters. Bea and Myles got to know them all. In the summers, the Kimmerly children delivered ice they'd cut from a nearby lake the winter before. Bea also took a job as clerk of the Omena Post Office, and when she retired in 1982, she was surprised to realize that she had worked there for twenty-six years.

In later life, Myles was elected Probate Judge, the last from Leelanau County who had never been a lawyer. But during his tenure he drew great respect from the community. So much so, that after he died in 1972, they named a county park for him near Maple City.

After a pause in our conversation, Bea said, "You know, I think I've seen more change in my lifetime than almost anyone." I couldn't dispute that. When she was a child there were very few automobiles. Her family's means of transportation was a horse.

Teams and wagons carried goods over unpaved roads, and schooners and steamers delivered their merchandise to Omena's docks. Yet Bea has lived to see a man walk on the moon and the exploration of Mars.

I asked her what brings the greatest pleasure now. "My family," she answered with a smile. She has five grandchildren and five great grandchildren. A bunch of them were at her home last summer for a two-week stay. They played in the sand on a nearby beach, swam, ran and whooped in her woods, and in the evenings, brought out the game boxes.

Not so long ago a friend told her she was worried about an impending visit from her grandchildren. "They'll mess up the house badly," she grumbled. "Oh, you're missing so much," Bea told her. "They'll grow up very fast. Enjoy them while you can. You can clean up the house anytime."

One evening, during their summer stay, as the children played in her home, Bea noticed that board games were spread over the entire living room floor. It made her feel warm inside, reminding her of those earlier times in her life when people could have great fun with so little. At the end of their vacation, as the children were leaving, Bea realized that during their fourteen-day stay, the TV set had not been turned on a single time. That made her feel wonderful!

Bea Kimmerly has lived ninety-seven years and understands what living is about. How does that old song go, "The best things in life are ...." Well, you know the rest. ⚜

Norm Wheeler

August 2008

He's a solidly-built fellow in his fifties with a thick head of curly, sandy-colored hair. He has blue eyes and a ready smile.

Norm lives in a home he built out of recycled materials in a forest between Glen Arbor and Empire. It was originally constructed as an octagon but it has been added to so many times that after twenty years it now has twelve sides!

Norm grew up a rural Michigan kid and attended Olivet College. He arrived there with a strong interest in literature and he thought he might become an English major. But a funny thing happened. He took a physics class from a professor who was so good at explaining things, Norm just kept enrolling in his courses, a path that led him all the way to the study of astronomy. When he graduated he had a double major, the unlikely combination of Physics and English! He earned a Master's Degree, and then asked himself, "What do I do with my life now?" Since he had no immediate answer, he decided bumming around Europe might be a good idea, and that's what he did. Norm had a number of adventures but one turn of fate worked out particularly well for him. In 1976, he found himself in Denmark teaching English as a second language, and while there he met a pretty grocer's daughter named Mimi. They married the next year and had two children, both born in Denmark.

In 1980 he got a phone call from his old physics prof at Olivet. It seemed there was a position open for someone who could teach English as well as Astronomy, that unusual combination of abilities that Norm had. He accepted and the young family spent a delightful two years there.

In 1982 they moved north. Norm taught English right here at Interlochen, filling in for a teacher who was on a sabbatical leave. During that time he learned of an ideal opening just up the road at the Leelanau School teaching, you guessed it, English and Astronomy. He took the job in 1984 and has been there ever since.

He's now also the Director of the Lanphier Observatory there on the campus.

You might say that's the story of a full life: father, homebuilder, teacher, astronomer … a packed agenda. Right? Well, Norm is not the type of guy who sits around collecting dust. He's also an accomplished actor, often performing with community theatre groups. On weekends you're likely to find him in a bar or club. But he's not a big drinker. You see, he plays the flugelhorn and trumpet with three different musical groups. Yet his biggest avocation at this time of the year is with the Beach Bards Bonfire. On Friday evenings from the summer solstice in June to late August, folks gather around a fire on the beach at the Leelanau School beside the observatory for the recitation of poetry, stories, and songs. The only rule is you must know the material by heart and perform it out loud. The goal is to preserve something we are in danger of losing, our oral tradition. It all starts at 8:30 with the Children's Hour. Norm rises and always recites a quatrain from Longfellow's poem of the same name:

> Between the dark and the daylight,
> When the night is beginning to lower,
> Comes a pause in the day's occupations
> That is known as the Children's Hour.

The children then perform … kids as young as four. Some are the children of children who came years ago.

The adult segment starts at 10:00 with an invocation to the muse of the oral tradition. It may be something from Homer or Black Elk or maybe one of the Irish poets. On a good evening perhaps one hundred people attend. This is the twentieth year of the Beach Bards Bonfires.

As if life weren't full enough at the Wheeler household, Mimi recently started a company aptly named "Grocer's Daughter's Chocolates." So while Norm is doing his thing, she is making delicious cordials.

I asked Norm what brings him joy. His first reply was about his family and the love they share. Then he said, "I'm lucky to live in a part of the world where I can be surrounded by so many creative people." After a pause he added, "I'm happy being a teacher. I was fortunate. I had great teachers who inspired me to follow in their footsteps. I can't describe the joy I feel as I see people's faces light up when they understand something for the first time."

Norm Wheeler, a guy who recites poetry on a beach beside an observatory, and sees nothing unusual in the juxtaposition. ⚴

Rebecca Lessard

October 2007

It was a bird that changed her life, a little red-tailed hawk that had been hit by a car and brought into the wildlife rescue center where she was volunteering.

I'll get to the story of that injured hawk in a minute or so. I had heard her give a speech and was so fascinated by what she had to say, I called her and asked if I could find out more about what makes her tick. "Sure," she answered, and then gave me the most complicated set of directions I'd heard in a long time. "Couldn't we just meet somewhere for coffee?" I asked. "I think it would be easier." "No," she replied, "You need to see my place and how it's laid out."

I set out with a map, my cell phone, and plenty of trepidation, but her directions proved to be perfect. Yes, there were lots of twists and turns as I headed in the general direction of Empire, then down a sandy two-track through a lush forest. I came into a clearing beside a lovely, secluded pond. I could see a charming small home on the shore plus a number of screened-in outbuildings tucked into the woods.

Rebecca Lessard came up a path to greet me. She was an energetic, sandy-haired, pleasant woman with an easy manner of speech. She wore jeans, work boots and a loose-fitting tank top. In conversation, I learned that her husband is a boat mechanic and that they have two college-age children. Years ago they were living in Minnesota and had run into tough times financially. Jobs were scarce. They decided they had to move but weren't sure where. They knew they wanted to live in a place that has snow for cross-country skiing and hills for biking. They got out a map, found Traverse City by chance, made a visit and never looked back.

Rebecca had been a biology major, and soon after settling into our area she volunteered at the wildlife rescue center I mentioned earlier, working with mammals. One day she opened up the place to find that injured red-tailed hawk. It was in a crate with an attached note from a co-worker asking her to take it to a nearby vet. Rebecca didn't feel very comfortable around birds so she called the other volunteers to see if she could get some help, but to no avail. Reluctantly she loaded the crate in her car and headed for the vet. Once there, to her horror, she realized that because of a lack of manpower, she was going to have to get the hawk out of the crate by herself! She gritted her teeth and did the job. "But once I held that injured bird in my arms," she says, "my life changed."

Soon thereafter, she began attending sessions in Michigan and elsewhere that dealt with the care of raptors. By the way, raptors are birds of prey: hawks, owls, eagles, vultures, falcons, northern harriers, and osprey.

At first, Rebecca opened a small operation to help injured and ill raptors. The demand was heavy. Then in 2001, she created a not-for-profit corporation and named it Wings of Wonder. It's funded mostly by donations and grants. She now averages about fifty birds a year. The outbuildings I noticed on her property are a hospital and eight aviaries, which the Lessards and volunteers have built.

Rebecca figures that in an average year she can release about 65% of the raptors that come her way. As for the rest, some simply don't recover and others have become too used to human contact to make it alone again in the wild. She keeps some of those as "ambassador birds." You see, Rebecca does about one hundred programs a year. She always takes a couple of raptors with her … perhaps an owl and a small hawk. She shows them to the audience as she delivers her message about wildlife conservation, ecology, and habitat preservation. Last year she figures she appeared before some nine thousand people.

Orphaned birds are also brought to Wings of Wonder. That's when some of the ambassador birds become foster moms. One owl has raised twenty-six orphan babies teaching them such things as flying and hunting skills.

All of this comes at a cost. Rebecca estimates it takes eight hundred hours to rehabilitate a raptor and there are expenses for food, medicine and electricity. Yet, there are great rewards. When the time arrives for a "release," Rebecca invites the public to witness the event. She puts out a message on her web site as well as informing the television and radio stations and the newspapers. Sometimes as many as five hundred people show up to watch as the bird soars to freedom once again.

I asked her how she feels when one of her birds is released. She replied, "Oh, it's the best. It's my inspiration."

After I left Rebecca, I realized I had another question, so I called her. "What ever happened to that first red-tailed hawk … the one that changed your life?" I asked. She replied that about six weeks after she first held it, she was able to release it back into the wild.

So, the next time you are walking in the woods or across a meadow and you see a hawk gliding on the wind high above, I hope you'll think about that red-tailed fellow, and of Rebecca Lessard. ⚶

Janet Weiler

AUGUST 2007

I'd heard she was quite the runner and that she was seventy-one years old! I wanted to meet her so I gave her a call. "Meet me at the Friendly Tavern," she said. "It's across the street from the Post Office in Empire."

I arrived for our appointment a bit early and walked in to grab a table. The bartender smiled. So did the waitresses. The place certainly did seem friendly.

Through the door came a trim little gray-haired woman wearing a tight black jacket, black stretch pants, and running shoes. It had to be Janet. "I hear you run marathons," I said. "And triathlons too," she replied. "Why?" I asked. "Because it's fun and I'm good at it," she answered.

"Do you like those shoes?" asked a friendly man at a nearby table who turned out to be her shoe salesman. "I love them," answered Janet. "I wore them in 'the Boston.' Came in fourth in my age group."

"When did you start running?" I asked.

"Four years ago."

"At age sixty-seven?"

"That's right," she answered.

I decided I should try to get some background and find out what would possess a woman of her age to take up such a grueling sport.

It turns out that Janet Weiler grew up in San Antonio. Her family summered in Michigan. Back then it took them seven days to drive from Texas to South Haven on two-lane roads all the way. She grew to adore the north.

She married and had three children whom she raised in Texas. The marriage ended after twenty-seven years, leaving Janet on her own. The children all had opted to attend the University of Michigan so she bought a small farm near Ann Arbor to be close to them. She settled in and got a job.

In 1994, taking some time off, she drove further north and happened on the sleepy village of Empire. It was autumn and she was enchanted by the beauty. She loved the fact that there were only a few people around. The kids had all graduated so she sold her Ann Arbor place, and moved to Empire, building a home on twenty acres in the midst of an old apple orchard.

In 2003 she visited a son, now a Chicago lawyer, and discovered he had embraced marathon running. He said, "You know mom, if you train you could run the twenty-six miles too." She laughed at the thought. "No," he said, "You really could do it." She thought it over and started an exercise regime, and later that year she and all three of her children ran in the Chicago Marathon.

"My time was embarrassing," she says, "over six hours. But I finished."

She continued to train, running at least nine miles a day, summer and winter, and began entering events all over the country.

This year, she returned to Chicago to run in the marathon once more. She ran the course an hour-and-a-half faster than her initial attempt and came across the finish line first in her age category.

As if marathons weren't tough enough, it was her children who convinced her to enter triathlons as well! In case you don't know what that is, it's a race in which typically you swim a mile, bike twenty-six miles, then finish up by running six miles. That, of course, means added training for Janet. For example, she regularly swims long distances in Lake Michigan from mid-May to late October. In addition, she does hard riding on her bicycle and runs doggedly on the trails of the nearby national park. The locals are used to seeing Janet training but not the tourists. An out-of-town couple recently ran in to Deering's Market in Empire to report they'd seen a woman way out in Lake Michigan who probably was in need of help. "Oh, don't worry" said the owner, "that's just Janet." In May, she participated in the Wildflower Triathlon at Monterey, California. Once more she won in her age category. Later she entered a half-marathon in Traverse City. It covered just over thirteen miles and is called the "Bay Shore." Again she came in first in her age group, finishing the course in two hours and five minutes. "Next time I'm in that race," she told me; "I'm going to go all out. I could have done better."

I was curious about where she found all the time to train and compete, so I asked her if she was retired. "Oh, no," she replied. "I inherited a little money but I need to work."

"Where?" I asked.

"Right here. I clean houses. I did one this morning," she answered.

"Are you as speedy about that job as you are with your running?"

She laughed and said, "This year at the Empire Asparagus Festival I wore a sign that read 'The Fastest Mop in Town.'"

I asked her about her goals in life. She told me she wanted to become faster in her racing. And then she added, "You know marathons are hard to do. In fact, they're horrible. But if they were easy, there'd be no glory in them. They are the poor man's version of climbing Mount Everest."

She paused and then said, "I never want to be DNF. Not in a race ... not in life."

"What is DNF?"

"Did Not Finish," she replied.

Abruptly Janet told me she had to leave. She was off for a long run with her dog. She looked out the window at the azure sky and observed that since the weather was good, she'd probably swim a few miles as well. She rose and moved quickly toward the door passing a friendly waitress. As I watched her go I realized I was exhausted but also uplifted. I thought to myself, "There goes some kind of seventy-one-year-old! I have no doubt that she really is the fastest mop in town." ⚑

Lisa Wehr

FEBRUARY 2008

I met her at the building she recently bought on the north edge of
Traverse City on M22. It's a modern, brown, three-story affair on
the shore of the bay. I was escorted
through a large open room where a
number of attractive, smiling people were working at computers. As
I entered a formal conference room
I was startled by a loud noise and
discovered it had come from a colorful parrot housed in a cage
just outside the door. Moments later, Lisa Wehr, a woman in her
mid-forties, came in with a stride that let me know immediately
who was in charge around there. Following her were two dogs that
seemed quite at home.

A question or two and out came her story. She'd attended a
community college in Florida where she was an honor student, but
she lacked sufficient funds and had to drop out before getting a
degree. She was able to find employment in a sheriff's office as a fo-
rensic photographer. For more than three years, Lisa shot pictures
of crime scenes, stings, and autopsies.

She moved to Ohio to be near family and to get married. She
began to develop an interest in dogs. A big interest! She acquired
ten of them! You see, she had become enamored with the idea of
shouting "Mush!" In the summer, she trained her team of sled dogs
on a cart with wheels. In the winter, she traveled to events in places
with snow like Grayling and Mt. Morris.

Soon Lisa had twenty-eight dogs and wanted more space and
an abundance of snow. She decided Kalkaska would be just right,
so she and her husband moved there. On a whim, they travelled
to Alaska to witness the famous Iditarod sled dog race. "It was a
mistake," she now says. That's because she loved the atmosphere so

much that on the day before they were to return, they put a down payment on a house. "I wasn't sure the check would clear," she told me softly. "We were living pretty much hand-to-mouth." I began to realize that Lisa was someone who was not afraid of taking chances.

Her husband got a job as an electrician. For the next six years she ran her dogs full-time, picking up a few sponsors. The races were four hundred miles long and she participated in fifty of them! She often finished in the top ten and sometimes she won, but Lisa and her husband were barely getting by financially. In addition to the costs of everyday living, she now owned some sixty dogs. Once in a while, she needed to call her parents for money.

Life might have continued in that fashion were it not for a near tragedy. It was March and the temperature was twenty-five degrees. She was racing at night. The route she chose led her up a frozen river. Suddenly Lisa, the dogs, and the sled plunged into open water. She thrashed about and was finally able to pull herself out onto the ice only to discover that the dogs were tangled in their lines, in danger of drowning. Somehow she got them all out and found shelter. It was her last race.

Soon after, Lisa discovered she was pregnant and as she puts it, "a light bulb went on." It was time for something different. She sold the dogs and went to a "big box" store, bought a computer and a book about how to use it. Soon she was competent enough to teach herself web design. Word of mouth spread, she started creating web sites for others, and she began making money. In fact, by the time her son was four, she was doing quite well. But the winters were getting long and she wanted to be near family again. Her parents were now living in Charlevoix, so Lisa sold her fledgling business and moved to nearby Traverse City. It seemed like a good place to live. In the year 2000, she opened up in a location on Park Drive, keeping the corporate name she had conceived in Alaska, "One Up Web." Sadly, the year 2000 also produced a divorce for her.

Search engine marketing became her focus. After a year she needed more space for employees and equipment so she bought a home in Suttons Bay that looked like it could house her and the business. It worked for a while but very quickly her company outgrew it too. Two more locations followed until she bought the building on the bay where she now runs her business. She thinks it should be big enough for a while with twenty-three thousand square feet of space!

One Up Web currently employs about forty people and serves clients across the nation. It has twice been named the "Best Search Engine Marketing Firm" in the country and in 2006 the Edward Lowe Foundation singled it out as "one of the top fifty companies to watch." That's pretty heady stuff for a woman who was mostly chasing sled dogs just fifteen years ago. She tosses that part off with a laugh. "It's true, I have lived," she told me, "but I wouldn't be as successful today if I hadn't done all those other things."

As I was leaving, I asked her why she kept the two dogs and the bird in offices of such a high tech operation. "Oh, that goes back to when we were working out of my home in Suttons Bay," she answered. "They are my house pets. Over time my employees came to consider them part of the family. Besides, Skippy the parrot doesn't like to be alone!"

Lisa Wehr. It's pretty clear she's a woman who hears her own drummer. ⚘

Lud Ashley

Sᴇᴘᴛᴇᴍʙᴇʀ 7, 2007

When I was planning this radio series, I decided that perhaps certain subject matter should be avoided ... you know, topics like politics, because they can sometimes be upsetting to people. Today as you listen to my yarn, you may think, for a while, that I've broken my own rule. But I believe you'll agree when I've finished that this is not really a story about politics at all. Instead, it's a story about a very special relationship.

His name is Thomas William Ludlow Ashley, but he goes by "Lud." He's a man of moderate build, thinning gray hair, with a pleasant, somewhat amused look on his face. Lud is no spring chicken. He's 84. Give him the "once over" and you can tell he stays in pretty good shape.

Lud lives in a charming white cottage on the Leland River. His wooded lot is punctuated with plantings of beautiful roses. On both sides of his front door there is red, white, and blue bunting. On the river side of the house, there is a wide, lovely porch — a wonderful spot to sit and watch the world drift by.

Lud grew up in Toledo, Ohio. His parents had once been comfortable but they were hurt badly by the Great Depression. Despite hard times they maintained a high regard for education and, through sacrifice, made certain their children got good ones. Lud and his brothers all attended prep schools. In 1941 Lud went to the Kent School in Connecticut ... and then, with some financial aid, he entered Yale University. He was there only a few months before being called into the army. He served in the field artillery in the Pacific.

In 1945 he went back to Yale. There he met another vet, a war hero named George. He, like many returning veterans was married. His wife's name was Barbara and they had a son who was a toddler. Lud and George (by the way his full name was George Herbert Walker Bush) hit it off and were soon fast friends. They joined the same fraternity and were inducted together into the Skull and Bones Society. Lud was a good student and played football. George starred in baseball and was a Phi Beta Kappa majoring in business.

They graduated in 1948. The Bushs returned to Texas, Lud to Toledo … and they vowed to remain in touch.

Back home Lud got to know and work for the mayor, Mike DiSalle. He grew to like Lud and urged him to go to law school. Lud did, finishing up at Ohio State and then practicing for about a year.

One day a friend from Yale contacted him and offered Lud a job in New York City working for Radio Free Europe. Getting news from the Free World to folks behind the Iron Curtain appealed to Lud and he accepted.

It was at this time that he and George saw each other again. The Bushs' small daughter, Robin, had contracted leukemia and they brought her to New York's Sloan-Kettering Hospital for treatment. The friends spent much time together during that tragic period. Lud often went to the hospital to check on the child. In fact, he visited so many times some of the staff thought he was a member of the family. Unfortunately, little Robin didn't make it, and the Bushs returned to Texas in deep sorrow.

At about the same time Lud heard from his Toledo mentor, Mike DiSalle. "Come back home," he said. "I think you should run for Congress."

Lud liked the idea. The year was 1954. The election turned out to be a three-way race. Lud says each candidate got 33% of the vote, but that he got 33% PLUS. Yes, he won in a "squeaker." It was the beginning of a long political career.

In 1964 George H. W. Bush was also elected to Congress. It was an occasion for a joyous reunion for the two men. In all, Lud would serve thirteen terms … and George H. W. Bush, as you know, went on to become our forty-first president.

Lud is proud of his accomplishments in Congress, particularly in the area of housing, but he's most proud of the things he could do for individuals. As a Congressman, he had the power to help people and he used it to change lives for the better.

He's also proud that he had good relationships with all of the presidents under whom he served: Eisenhower, Kennedy, Johnson, Nixon, Carter, and of course, especially with his old, good friend, George H. W. Bush. When Lud's wife Kathleen died ten years ago, the Bushes were at the funeral in Washington. Lud was in attendance two years ago when the aircraft carrier *George Herbert Walker Bush* was christened. He was invited to the Bush's 50th wedding anniversary celebration. On his pal's 80th birthday they parachuted over Texas.

In her recent book, *My Father, My President*, Doro Bush Koch mentions Lud some thirty times.

Lud and George are still in touch with each other at least once a week by phone or email. The thought of that relationship brings a warm smile to Lud's face as he sits there on his porch overlooking the Leland River.

And so, that's my story for today. Oh, except there is a bit of a twist. As we all know George H. W. Bush is a Republican. But perhaps you didn't know, Lud Ashley, the thirteen-term Congressman from Ohio, he's a Democrat.

So you see, this isn't really a story about politics. It's a story of friendship … a story about how things once were in this country and, in my view, how they should be again. ⚓

Dreamers

We don't have eternity to realize our dreams –
only the time we are here.

Susan L. Taylor

> I prefer to be a dreamer among the
> humblest, with visions to be realized,
> than lord among those without
> dreams or desires.
>
> Kahlil Gibran

You may say that I'm a dreamer,
But I'm not the only one.
I hope some day you'll join us,
And the world will live as one.

John Lennon

> We are the music makers,
> And we are the dreams we dream.
> Wandering by lone sea breakers;
> And sitting by desolate streams.
> World losers and world foresakers
> For whom the pale moon gleams.
> Yet we are movers and the shakers
> Of the world forever it seems.
>
> Arthur William Edgar O'Shaughnessy

Sharon Sutterfield

November 2006

She is a vivacious woman who is just old enough to be beyond her mid-life crisis. She's tall in stature, has carrot-red hair, and bursts into a hearty laugh at the drop of a hat. That's because she's happy. However, that was not always the case. Let's go back a bit.

For a number of years Sharon lived downstate in upscale Auburn Hills. Starting in the mid-'70s, she worked for an automotive manufacturer who made interiors. She handled the Chrysler account.

Sharon was good at her job and could afford a nice lifestyle. Oh, there was a failed romance along the way, and there were some nagging health problems, but for the most part there were few bumps in the road. Yet, after twenty-two years on the job, she began to feel restless. That feeling grew into a full-blown determination to do something else, like running her own business.

Several years earlier, Sharon had driven north for a vacation and found Leelanau County. She loved what she saw and experienced there. Those memories lingered, so in the spring of 1998, she headed back north with the intention of finding a path to a new life.

Once in Leelanau County, she took a deep breath of fresh air and began to search out options. She looked, and she looked, but she found nothing. Well, not really nothing. A baker offered her the job of getting his sour dough started every day at 5:00 AM! It was the kind of opportunity that made her old occupation look pretty good.

Sharon was about to give up and return to Auburn Hills. It was a Sunday morning. She decided to make one more swing through the county. She was on the road to Northport when she happened to glance down at her fuel gauge. It was one of those shocking moments that everyone dreads. Her tank was so empty, she figured she must have been driving on fumes. What to do? It was Sunday. The only gas station that she knew was about eight or ten miles behind her in Suttons Bay.

Sharon immediately turned around and hoped for the best. Fortunately she made it into the village, but just barely. Her engine died and the car coasted to a stop at the curb in front of a quaint lodge-like building with an exterior that looked to have been constructed with fieldstones. A sign in front read "Korner Kottage." Another sign caught her eye as well: "Open House – For Sale." Sharon climbed out of her lifeless automobile and went inside. She discovered that the place was absolutely charming, and that it was a bed and breakfast. Instantly, she knew what she was going to do. She was going to buy it.

Now, that was a rather remarkable decision for Sharon to make, in that she had no experience running a B&B. In fact, she'd never even stayed in one. Because of her work in the automotive industry, she did know that she had business and people skills. She also knew how to cook. That's what she had to go on, and as rash as it sounds, she drove home, drew up a business plan and made an offer. Within thirty days, the deal was complete. Seventeen days after that, Sharon Sutterfield was open for business as the new owner and operator of The Korner Kottage in Suttons Bay.

That was some eight years ago. The place has hummed along very nicely ever since. In recent months, however, Sharon began to get that restless feeling again. She had no desire to leave this part of Michigan, but she'd begun taking decorating assignments on the side, and found that her work was appreciated. So, very recently, she sold her B&B, to open a new interior design business.

"Where will you live?" I asked.

"Temporarily, with a friend," she replied. "Then I'll find a house."

"Where?" I wondered.

"Oh, I don't know," she answered. "Somewhere close by. I haven't a clue right now."

"I've got an idea," I told her. "Why don't you get into your car and drive around until you run out of gas? It worked the last time!"

She laughed and replied, "You know, I might just do that." ⚘

Mike Grosvenor

NOVEMBER 2008

In the summertime, when he was a little boy, Mike Grosvenor often stayed at his grandparents' home on South Manitou Island. He remembers that as he lay in the darkness trying to fall asleep, the beam from the island's lighthouse would shine through the window and fall across his bed. It was a lovely way to drift off, an image he would never forget.

Today, Mike is fifty-nine and has the ruddy complexion of someone who spends lots of time out-of-doors. I sought him out because he's the third generation of his family to own and run the boat service to and from the Manitou Islands. I thought he might have a yarn or two to share.

First, some background: the Manitous lie offshore from the Leelanau Peninsula in Lake Michigan. North Manitou is twelve-and-a-half miles out from Leland ... South is sixteen. They guard the famous Manitou Passage, a popular lane for commercial shipping. It's used because the islands provide protection from the prevailing westerly winds and also because it's a shortcut. That's the upside. The downside: the passage is only about a mile wide and there are many dangerous shoals to navigate. That's why, in the 1830's a lighthouse was constructed on South Manitou.

Today, the islands are part of the Sleeping Bear National Lakeshore and are uninhabited. But during the lumbering days, those islands hummed with activity. On North there was a town that boasted a population of three hundred. South had two villages and a population of one hundred ten at the turn of the century.

Mike's great-grandfather worked as a sawyer on North Manitou. His grandfather and father were born there. In the early days, a man from Glen Haven had a contract with the U.S. Postal Service to run mail daily to and from South Manitou. But in 1913, his boat was wrecked in a storm. Mike's grandfather owned a boat, saw an opportunity, got the contract, and began servicing both islands. He carried the mail as well as crops, supplies, and people between the islands and Leland.

In 1871, a tower and new light were added to the old 1830's lighthouse. George's grandfather often steered by that light and so did his father who took over the business and ran it for fifty years. Young Mike started early in the family operations. He learned on the job. He likes to recall the tale that in 1963, family members drove him to Detroit to bring back a new boat. Although he was old enough to pilot a boat (and could do so with skill) he had to be driven because he was too young to get an automobile driver's license.

Mike went away to college but spent his summers in the family business. When his schooling ended, he folded right in.

In 1958, the Coast Guard turned off the South Manitou light. It was replaced by an automated one erected on a "crib" between the two islands.

In 1982, Mike took over, operating two large boats to and from both islands every day during the summer season. After the Park Service assumed control of the islands, the need for mail stopped. There were no permanent residents any more. But Mike thrived, ferrying day hikers and campers.

Each morning, his boats depart at 10:00 and return in the late afternoon. It means that Mike spends every day on South Manitou. But he doesn't waste his time. He has steeped himself in its knowledge and lore and, using dune buggies, he conducts tours. He shows his guests the virgin cedar forest, which contains our nation's oldest, and largest white cedar trees. He points out the wreck of the *Francisco Morizon*, the 360-foot freighter that ran aground during a November blizzard in 1960. And for years, as he has taken his guests to the old white lighthouse standing abandoned on the eastern shore, he has felt a twinge of nostalgia.

Then, a couple of years ago, something happened that began to lift his spirits. It seemed that others missed the old light as well.

A group was formed (Mike among them) named The Manitou Islands Memorial Society. They looked around for money to restore the light. They learned the National Park Service was soon to celebrate its one-hundredth anniversary. In fact, their "Centennial Initiative," as it was called, would match funds for historical projects such as this one.

Mike's group came up with more than $45,000 in donations and the National Park Service provided most of the rest. A replica of the original giant lens was made, the lantern room in the building was refurbished, and last summer the new light was installed.

On a late September evening, Mike was in a crowd gathered on a beach at Glen Haven with a clear view of South Manitou. As dusk descended they waited and watched. Then suddenly … there it was. The light from South Manitou winked on after half a century of darkness. I can only imagine what Mike's feelings were, seeing it once again; the light that had guided his grandfather, his father, Mike, and now will guide his own children. The beam that had fallen across his childhood bed on South Manitou was there once more.

Mike Grosvenor is someone who understands, in a very moving way, "what goes around, comes around." ⚓

John Scott

January 2012

Last autumn, at a fund-raiser for the Old Art Building in Leland, a raffle was held. I had promised that I would write an episode of "The Story Next Door" about whoever drew the winning ticket. It would be a test of my tenet that everyone has a good tale to tell. A man named John Scott won.

I knew him by sight only. He's hard to miss. He cuts a commanding figure. From fall through late spring he wears a beret and an impressive scarf tied like a cravat. He has white hair, a neatly trimmed white beard, and his blue eyes shine from behind horn-rimmed glasses.

I called John and told him we had to get together because he held the winning raffle ticket. I got directions and drove over to see him on a lovely afternoon last October. I discovered he lives in the country not far from the village of Lake Leelanau. His roadside mailbox reads "Provemont Hill Vineyard." I turned up his dirt lane. On my left, sloping down a hillside, I saw grapevines covered with white netting that prevents birds from eating the ripe fruit.

I inched up a steep incline through woods, and then to the right I saw his home. It was something you might find at a ski resort in Colorado, lodge-like and yet contemporary. It commands beautiful views of farmland and orchards.

As I arrived, John was standing on a deck above me near his front door. In a deep voice he called for me to come on up.

"I saw your vineyard," I said. "Are you a winemaker?"

"I don't make it commercially," he answered. "I sell my grapes to local vintners."

We settled into the comfortable living area of the home. I learned that he is seventy-two, has been happily married for fifty years, and that he and his wife Mary have two grown sons.

John Scott's story unfolded. He was raised in Kalamazoo. His mother dabbled in art as a self-taught watercolor painter. She was enough of an influence on John that he began to paint as a child.

As he approached college age, he announced to his parents that he planned to embark on a career as an artist. They were horrified! His mother told him, "If you become a painter, you'll never be able to put orange juice on the table."

So John, with more than a little regret, took her advice. He attended the University of Michigan and graduated from the law school there. Eventually he and his wife settled in Kalamazoo where he became an expert lawyer dealing in trusts and estates.

During that period, he bought a cottage on Crystal Lake. The Scotts loved their northern Michigan times together.

One of John's favorite activities is hiking. The family has done it here on the mainland and on Beaver Island as well as in far-flung places like Tuscany, England, and Scotland.

John also had a latent interest in agriculture. Perhaps that was because one of his grandfathers was a carpenter and avid gardener. The other was a combination minister/farmer. As an adult, John dreamed that someday he would plant a vineyard.

John liked his work as a lawyer but his pastimes were beckoning. So, some sixteen years ago, when the Kalamazoo firm he worked for dissolved, John was faced with a choice: he could still bring in a comfortable living as a downstate lawyer, or he could take the firm's closing as a sign to make a change. He did the latter. He opened a small practice in Traverse City, and shortly thereafter, he and Mary bought the land on which they now live. He indeed planted his vineyard and has returned to his first love of painting. He does it almost every day. His watercolors are very special.

It all sounds remarkably simple. Doesn't it? Well, it wasn't. I discovered that when I asked John a question: "Is there any one thing that changed your life?" Without hesitation, he answered, "Hiking the Appalachian Trail." Then he digressed. He told me that initially, the idea of actually leaving Kalamazoo was not easy. He and Mary were comfortable there. "But," he told me, "I had strong forces pulling at me, dreams that were instilled in me: nature, painting, farming. Yet I still needed to make something of a living and I worried because Traverse City already had plenty of lawyers.

Would there be room for me there too? Could Mary and I find happiness full-time in the Northland?"

But John had learned a valuable lesson some years before. In his early fifties, he felt the need to clear his head. For a long while, he had dreamed of hiking the Appalachian Trail. He told his firm he needed time off, a big chunk of time. His colleagues resisted but John threw caution to the wind and did it anyway. He grabbed his pack and headed south to test himself. The Appalachian Trail meanders through mountains and wilderness from northern Georgia to northern Maine. John endured the aches of muscles and the pains of blisters. He kept a wary eye out for bear, wild boar, and poisonous snakes. He hiked, off and on, for some three months. Every day he had to make essential decisions about food, water, and shelter. "Putting one foot in front of the other for fifteen hundred miles was a remarkable experience," he told me. "Up to that time, I had taken few real risks in my life. But I wanted to do something very basic and confront my fears." When it was over, John discovered it had been a life-changing experience.

So, years later, when confronted with the dilemma of cutting ties in Kalamazoo, John was prepared. He drew on what he had learned from the experience on the Appalachian Trail, and chose opportunity over security. He made the decision and has not looked back.

At the end of our visit, I realized I was glad to have met John Scott … a guy who was willing to take a big chance in life. He also took a chance when he bought a raffle ticket … and that's how I got the chance to find and tell his story. ⚘

Bill Livingston

AUGUST 2011

Today's chapter fits the adage "The apple doesn't fall far from the tree."

I drove north on country roads in the direction of Northport on the Leelanau Peninsula. I had an appointment with a man named Bill Livingston. I turned up a forest lane and saw his neat, rustic home tucked into a clearing. Colorful flowerbeds edged the yard.

I found Bill in his workshop on the ground level of the house. He is a tall, lean man who wears glasses and has a mustache that matches his brown hair. He appears younger than his sixty-eight years.

We climbed the stairs to the living area of his home. It's constructed of wood and stone that give it a warmth that seems just right for a home in the forest. He and his wife Judy built it with their own hands in 1978, the year they were wed.

It's been a loving marriage that has produced one daughter who currently attends college in the Pacific Northwest.

Bill's father, for whom he was named, had been well educated with a degree in botany from the University of Wisconsin, but he preferred working with his hands to the scholar's life. When Bill was born, his dad was employed at a Chicago shipyard helping build large yachts.

The family spent a few summer vacations in northern Michigan and liked it so much, they decided to live here. They moved to Northport in 1951. That's where Bill and his three sisters grew up. His father wanted to build wooden sailboats for a living. He set up shop in a long narrow shed next to the harbor.

Bill's dad turned out to be a magnificent craftsman, and quite a character. Summer and winter he worked in his bare feet. He was innovative. He made his lead keels in a salvaged bathtub. He cut Osage Orange from a nearby hedge to construct his tillers. No detail was too small. Around town he became known as a good conversationalist, a kind of philosopher. He always seemed to have a cigarette between his lips.

Bill estimates his father made about thirty boats. They were highly prized by their owners and Bill knows for sure that some are still in use. But the most special one he ever built was made as a gift for his wife. It was a racing sloop — long, lean, and fast — perfectly designed for the protected waters of Northport Bay. He named it *Witchcraft*. "My mother was happiest when sailing," Bill told me. "The boat was a perfect fit for her. She just loved it."

I asked him if it still exists. "Yes," he replied. "It's being restored by the Maritime Heritage Alliance in Traverse City. It's of great historic value, one of a kind."

Bill's father doted on his daughters, but he and his son never saw eye-to-eye. "I was afraid of him," Bill told me. "He was there but I knew it wasn't welcoming territory" As a result, Bill was never able to apprentice with his father.

So, young Bill turned away, deciding he'd become a scholar. He earned a bachelor's and a master's degree and got a job at Traverse City Central High School teaching chemistry. He taught for eight years. Yet he was restless. He enjoyed the kids but not the job. Like his father before him, he yearned to work with his hands.

Suddenly, at the age of fifty-eight, his father died of complications from emphysema. Bill said, "I was thirty when he passed away. I never made peace with him. I wish I had. Now, I kind of deify him."

At about the time of his father's death, Bill quit teaching and took up a career in carpentry. He quickly discovered the work suited him, and he pursued it for more than three decades. He retired a couple of years ago … with a dream. He wanted to build a boat, a replica of the one his dad had built for his mother.

And there in his workshop I saw it. He's been working on it for a year-and-a-half with about six months left to go. The wooden sloop is twenty-four feet long, six feet wide, with a draft of four feet. It will carry two sails and will weigh just over two tons. In fact, it's so big that Bill will have to remove a wall to get it out of his shop.

The workmanship is beautiful, done with the same artistry his father used. And there is one very special touch. When his father died, and the family closed his workshop, they took his supply of mahogany and stored it under their home. Bill recently retrieved it and is using it to trim his boat "Dad never had a lot of money," Bill explained. "So I look at the mahogany as my inheritance. To see it gracing this sloop just makes me feel good."

I asked him what he was going to do with the finished boat. "I'm going to give it to my wife," he answered. "She's given me so much. I want to express my gratitude and love. It will be hers."

There is some irony here. In spite of the fact that Bill Livingston and his dad were not close, in so many ways, "Like father, like son." ⚓

Heroes

A hero is an ordinary individual who
finds the strength to persevere and
endure in spite of overwhelming obstacles.

CHRISTOPHER REEVE

We can't all be heroes because
somebody has to sit on the curb and
clap as they go by.

WILL ROGERS

Bob Maynard

April 2008

He lives with his wife just outside of Suttons Bay in a cottage set in a grove at the water's edge. He's a guy of average height with a rugged build. When you speak to him his eyes remain on you intently. That's because he has to work hard to hear. His eardrums were damaged years ago by a loud explosion. Bob Maynard will turn eighty-eight this year.

He grew up in Cleveland, Ohio and went to Albion College. There he started off well, but something happened in his junior year. He's not sure what it was, perhaps too much social life, but his grades went downhill so badly that he quit, not knowing what to do next. It was 1941. One week after he got home, Pearl Harbor was attacked. Then he immediately knew what to do. He headed for a recruiting office.

However, Bob had some physical problems. The Navy turned him down. Flat feet. The Air Corps followed suit. Bad eyes. So did the Marines. Heart murmur. Finally he went to the Army. There a doctor simply asked, "Can you touch your toes?" When Bob accomplished that, the doctor said, "Fine. You're in." That was the total extent of his physical exam.

He was sent to Officers Training School and emerged a second lieutenant in October of 1942. He married his sweetheart Betty while on leave. Soon after, he was sent to Italy and had his baptism by fire on the beach at Anzio. Later he took part in another landing on a beach in France, south of Normandy. He fought across France and Germany in a Tank Destroyer Battalion. Finally, as the war was nearing its end, he found himself at Hitler's country retreat, the Eagle's Nest in Austria. He was among the first American soldiers to walk through the empty, litter-strewn estate.

In all of his war adventures, Bob never got a scratch, yet he survived six extremely close calls, including the time he stepped on a land mine. He simply heard a click as it misfired.

In his march across Europe, he had gotten to know a young infantryman named Audie Murphy. "When I first met him he was a seventeen-year-old kid," Bob told me. "He weighed about one hundred twenty pounds. I don't even think he shaved yet!" He added that Murphy was a sharpshooter who was absolutely fearless.

One day, as the platoon of tank destroyers approached a small village, Bob peered through his field glasses and saw German tanks in the streets. A battle began. Bob's company commander was seriously wounded and Bob was immediately promoted to captain. He took over as company commander with three platoons serving under him.

The battle was fierce and three of Bob's tank destroyers were disabled. As the Germans advanced en masse, Audie Murphy jumped to the deck of one of the wrecked vehicles where there were three working machine guns. Completely exposed to the Nazi guns he began to fire, mowing down the oncoming enemy. He was wounded twice but kept on shooting. His courage and skill were essential in repelling the German advance. For his brave act, Audie Murphy was later awarded the Congressional Medal of Honor. Bob is still proud of the fact that he was part of that fight and witness to Murphy's courage.

When Bob finally got back to Cleveland, he had spent some three hundred days on the front lines. He finished his college education and subsequently had a thirty-year career with General Motors. He retired in 1980 and, with their five children grown, Bob and Betty moved to their cottage on Grand Traverse Bay. They will celebrate their sixty-fifth wedding anniversary this year.

These days, as Bob reflects, there are thousands of memories, yet one seems to stand out over the rest. While he was fighting in Germany, his first child was born, a little girl. On his return, he couldn't wait to see her for the first time. She was now thirteen months old. When he went to his home, Betty and a group of relatives greeted and hugged him. They all wanted to go up to the baby's room together to witness the emotional event. But Betty said firmly, "No. This needs to be just for the three of us." The couple climbed the stairs and tiptoed toward the room. Bob slid through the doorway and saw his daughter standing up in her crib. There was a picture of Bob on the wall beside her. Betty pointed to Bob and said quietly, "Barbara, here's daddy." The child looked at Bob, then at the picture on the wall, then back to Bob … and opened her arms to him. Still, sixty-four years after that moment, the memory brings tears to Bob's eyes.

An American hero… a loving father … Bob Maynard. ⚜

Jerry Linenger

January 2008

People find the Northland in a variety of ways, some quite unusual. But none can beat how Jerry Linenger discovered this part of the world.

He's fifty-three now — tan, trim, active, clearly a jock. I'm going to pick up Jerry's story when he was fourteen. It was July of 1969. He and his family were taking a vacation trip, staying at a campground on the shores of Lake Huron. As the sun was setting, Jerry and his older brother were sprawled on a sand dune watching the moon rise. On that evening, the sight was particularly thrilling for them because they knew that American astronauts were up there. The boys raced back to the camp where someone had set up a small black and white television set on a picnic table. Jerry watched Neil Armstrong and Buzz Aldrin plant an American flag on the surface of the moon. He looked on as Walter Cronkite, awestruck, reported the historic event. It was at that moment that Jerry made up his mind. Someday he was going to be an astronaut. It was a wonderful dream for a boy to have, but little did he know how difficult the odds were for reaching a goal like that.

Jerry was a good student and had every intention of going to college, but things were tight at home budget-wise. His dad worked as a telephone repairman, and with two older sisters and a brother already in college, tuition for Jerry seemed a stretch. However, an observant congressman came to the rescue, offering Jerry an appointment to the U. S. Naval Academy. When his parents learned that if he entered Annapolis they would pay neither tuition nor room-and-board, the decision was a no-brainer. As for Jerry, he was thrilled because he knew that the majority of astronauts had graduated from the Academy.

He was also aware that astronauts came from a wide variety of backgrounds and academic specialties. As he matured, he understood that it was a long shot and he should prepare himself with an alternative plan. Becoming a flight surgeon seemed a good idea. "I just decided to do what interested me and to do it well," he told me. So he was pre-med at Annapolis, graduating third in a class of more than a thousand midshipmen.

As he had planned, he earned his MD, served as a flight surgeon, and along the way picked up two master's degrees and a Ph. D.

Then at the age of thirty-seven, Dr. Jerry Linenger was indeed selected to become an astronaut. He and his wife Kathryn moved to Houston. Two years later, he flew aboard the Shuttle Discovery completing one hundred seventy-seven orbits. Upon his return, he was assigned to Russia to prepare to re-enter space with two Cosmonauts heading for the Space Station Mir. It meant he would have to become fluent in Russian and learn all of the Mir systems.

On January 12, 1997, Linenger launched aboard the U.S. Space Shuttle Atlantis, linking up with Mir, where he was to remain for nearly five months. During that time he became the first American to conduct a space walk from a foreign station in a non-American space suit. His space walk lasted five hours.

While aboard Mir, Jerry and the Russians faced a number of serious challenges, including loss of electrical power, loss of orientation control resulting in a dizzying tumble through space, and the most serious fire ever aboard a spacecraft. Jerry played a major role in helping overcome those mishaps, all the while communicating only in Russian.

I asked him about lessons learned on his journey. His first response was about the value of his family and how much he loved them. The second was how he appreciated our beautiful and precious Earth that lay below him. He realized that, just as he was orbiting in a closed ecosystem that one dare not dramatically disturb, so was our world a closed ecosystem ... and the same lesson applied.

Aboard Mir, Jerry logged fifty million miles, more than two thousand orbits around the Earth at an average speed of eighteen thousand miles an hour. He had decided he wanted to use his time on Mir to become a world-class geographer. As a result, he took more than ten thousand photographs from space (many of which have become classics) and he observed and memorized the features of the world. He compiled a list of his five favorite places on the planet: the Himalayas, the Great Barrier Reef, the Caribbean, Japan and the northwest section of Michigan. Yes, he could see it clearly from space: Lake Michigan, Grand Traverse Bay, and Traverse City at night. He knew he would be retiring from the Navy in the near future and he realized he had become enamored with our part of the globe.

Jerry left the Navy in 1998. He and Kathryn had lived in wonderful parts of Texas and California, but he told the Navy to take their belongings to a warehouse in Traverse City, Michigan. "I'm going to find a place within one hundred miles of there," he informed them.

When I met him, it was at his lovely home on Suttons Bay. It's the place where the Linengers and their four children find great happiness. He has written a book about his adventures, gives motivational speeches around the country, is a consultant to the Discovery Channel on an upcoming Mars project, and appears regularly on NBC as a space expert. He also gives time to a variety of organizations and causes he deems important.

"What would you like your children to become in life?" I asked him. "I'll tell them to do what interests them and to do it well," he repeated. Then he added. "I did take them to Florida not long ago to witness a launch."

"I assume you haven't told them that the sky's the limit?" I asked.

"No, I haven't," he replied quietly. ⚓

Bob Willard

DECEMBER 2010

Today's chapter goes under the heading of, "Some Surprises Are Better than Others."

I see him regularly on the golf course. These days he often plays by himself. His name is Bob Willard. He is slim, white-haired, and always nattily dressed.

Bob grew up in a small town in western Pennsylvania. His father had only an eighth-grade education. The family was not well-to-do. They never owned a home or a car. Bob was a good student, but didn't really think of getting a college education. His folks simply didn't have the means for that. However, his intelligence caught the attention of his high school biology teacher, Miss Cline. She was a graduate of a college in northern Ohio. In his senior year she pulled him aside and announced, "Robert, you are going to go to my school, Oberlin College."

Miss Cline knew there were financial limitations. So she began a rigorous six-week tutoring regimen in hopes of getting Bob ready to take a test and win a scholarship. He passed with flying colors, was awarded twelve hundred dollars to cover four years of tuition and entered Oberlin in the fall of 1938. It was the first time he'd ever been away from home alone. Six weeks into his first semester he was summoned to the dean's office. "Uh, oh," thought Bob, "What have I done?" The dean stated that he'd received a call from his father. "He hasn't heard from you," the dean stated. "Your father wants to know if you're still in school!" Bob had been so caught up in academic life, he'd forgotten to call home.

At Oberlin, he entered the pre-med program. One day he met a pretty zoology major named Virginia and that lit a spark. They began to date. During his senior year, he applied to the Western Reserve Medical School and was accepted. But again ... how to pay for it? Virginia's father, a physician, came to his aid with a loan.

At the end of his first year, the military drafted his entire medical school class. Bob entered the Army Air Corps where he served as a flight surgeon for five years. It was during that time that he and Virginia married.

Next, he attended the Northwestern School of Medicine in Chicago. This time, the G. I. Bill paid his tuition. He did his residency in ophthalmology, earning a handsome salary of fifty dollars a month! During this time, he treated all kinds of patients, rich and poor. And he also had his share of adventures. He once was called in the middle of the night to rush to a Chicago hotel room to remove a cigarette ash from Frank Sinatra's eye. On another occasion, Carol Channing, who was appearing in a play, came into the emergency room in great pain. A contact lens was stuck under her eyelid. Bob fixed the problem and was given a pair of posh tickets to her show. George Halas, the legendary coach of the Chicago Bears, had lived his life with one crossed eye. Bob was part of a team that successfully operated to straighten it, and for that they received a Soldier Field box on the fifty-yard line.

With his residency complete, Bob and Virginia headed for Toledo, Ohio, her hometown, where Bob opened a practice which turned out to be a wonderful success. His skill as an ophthalmologist became widely known. So did his demeanor. He was just a nice guy. The Willards' marriage was also a success. They were a close and loving couple. Each respected the other's abilities and intellect. They were blessed with the births of four daughters.

They found their way to Leelanau County in the sixties and bought a beautiful lakefront lot north of Leland. In 1968 they built a home on it, which they used as a cottage for years. In 1989 he retired and they moved there full time.

Bob has spent his life caring for others ... and he hasn't stopped in retirement. He just accomplishes it in other ways. Sometimes neighbors and friends need a bit of medical advice or perhaps some emergency treatment. He is always there for them. When a new minister arrived at his church, Bob paid him a visit at his newly purchased home. Bob noticed that the yard was rather empty so he paid to have it landscaped. He's become close to the grounds crew at his golf club. When he learned that one of them was seriously ill and without the means to afford medical attention, Bob dipped into his own pocket and took care of the bill.

About four years ago, Bob began to notice a change in Virginia. A doctor's diagnosis revealed Parkinson's disease. That progressed into dementia. He cared for her at home for a few years, and then she had to be placed in a facility that offered assisted living. That's where she resides today.

Bob remains in the lakefront home. He reads, goes to movies, concerts, and regularly attends an exercise class ... but he admits that sometimes he's a bit lonely. That's why he thoroughly enjoys visits from his far-flung family. Last April, a daughter and her husband were at his home when a Sheriff's Department squad car pulled into his driveway. Bob rushed out saying, "If you're giving me a ticket just hand it over. I have visitors." "No," said the officer, "I have a summons. Get in your car and follow me to the Riverside Inn."

Bob did as instructed, bringing his visiting family with him. "I don't think the Inn is open at this time of year," he said. When they arrived, the officer escorted them in. A look of shock crossed Bob's face, followed by a smile. The room was filled with family: daughters, grandchildren, great grandchildren, and about fifty of his friends. A band was playing. The surprise was complete. Bob was surrounded by those who loved him, and his spirits were lifted ... at just the right time. Bob was turning ninety.

As I said at the beginning, some surprises are better than others. ⚘

Dick Grout

MAY 2011

He is not a big man, but for a ninety-year-old, he makes a very strong impression with his deep voice and strong New England accent. He also has a good, dry sense of humor that reflects that part of the country. Dick Grout and his wife live on the north side of Suttons Bay in a lovely new home on a hill overlooking the water.

He grew up in Wellesley, Massachusetts, home of the prestigious women's college. He graduated from Brown University in 1942. World War II was in high gear so he enlisted in the army. He was sent to Officers Training School and then shipped out to England as a Second Lieutenant. There he became a Platoon Commander in an Engineer Combat Battalion and prepared for the Allied invasion of Europe. He and his men practiced landings, building bridges, removing and laying mines.

One weekend he attended an English country fair. There he met a pretty Scottish lass named Norma who was a WAAF — a member of the female auxiliary of the Royal Air Force. He was smitten! He learned she was stationed on a base forty miles from his, so when he was granted an occasional pass, he would visit her, riding eighty miles round-trip on a bicycle! Talk about smitten! He proposed. She accepted, although both knew there could be no wedding until the war's end.

On June 6, 1944, he and his platoon of combat engineers were aboard landing craft headed for Omaha Beach as part of the first waves. They were assigned to remove obstacles on the shore so troops could land more safely. Their mission was also to destroy a wall the Germans had constructed to seal off an exit road from the beach. Under intense fire they accomplished both assignments. In his battalion of about two hundred men who landed that day, thirty-four were seriously wounded and thirty-seven killed. Later, Dick and his men felt great satisfaction watching Allied tanks and trucks move through the wall they had breached and head inland.

In the first months after the invasion his engineers had to work with whatever materials they could find. On one occasion, in France, they were sent to a canal that American forces needed to cross. The retreating Germans had destroyed the only bridge. Dick noticed a nearby furniture factory and, upon inspection, discovered a large supply of logs. Mahogany logs! He confiscated them and his men built a very sturdy bridge. It provided safe passage for the troops, and left behind one very exasperated French furniture maker. For all Dick knows, that mahogany bridge may still be standing.

Just before the Battle of the Bulge, Dick and his men were building another bridge while under German mortar fire. Dick was hit by shrapnel, hospitalized in England, and then returned to action. By the time Nazi Germany collapsed he had reached the rank of Major and he returned to Great Britain to find Norma. They were married in Dumfries, Scotland in the church where the poet Robert Burns had once belonged.

Back in the United States, Dick took a position with Mercer, the world's largest human resource consulting firm. He was assigned to the Detroit office where he worked with large pension plans. The couple lived in Orchard Lake, a small town near Bloomfield Hills. His career proceeded nicely. They had three children. Then as something of a surprise, he was named mayor of Orchard Lake. He took it in stride. After all, there couldn't be many problems in a town of around two thousand souls. That was true, until one day the Village Clerk called saying that he needed to perform a marriage. "What?" Dick yelled. "It's part of the job," the Clerk replied. Dick took a deep breath and performed the task. Before he left office, he officiated at weddings about ten more times!

In 1965, the Grouts bought a ramshackle farmhouse near Omena as a second home. For years, summer and winter, they worked at remodelling it. When Dick retired in 1982, they moved there permanently and opened an antique shop in Suttons Bay. It was a lovely life, until the day that Norma, a smoker, was diagnosed with lung cancer. Just one year later she was dead. Dick was devastated. He sold the shop and began to get deeply involved with community work. One evening, friends took him to a potluck supper where they had arranged for him to meet a pretty widow named Marion. Dick and Marion are now celebrating their twenty-fifth anniversary.

I asked him about the turning points in his life. He mentioned the births of his children and the death of Norma. He also talked about the joys of his second marriage. Then his thoughts turned to the War. "I had never seen death before," he said. "Then I suddenly saw a lot of it. But I wasn't psychologically damaged by the War. I knew our whole country was behind us. I just felt I had to do it. Get through it. Get it done. And that I did."

I should end there, but if you remember, I told you Dick has a good sense of humor. As I was leaving, I glanced at my notes. "Let's see," I said. "You grew up in Wellesley, Massachusetts. Right?"

"Yes."

"And you went to Brown University?"

"Yes, but it wasn't my first choice. I wanted to go to Wellesley, but I couldn't pass the physical." ⚶

Ted Lanham

March 2012

It might seem odd to think of the Fourth of July at this time of the year, but on these dark, frosty days, the idea of summer is refreshing. So my thoughts have turned to the annual celebration of the birth of our country … and to a small town parade.

In the village of Leland, it's a wonderfully old-fashioned event. Hours before it begins, folks start gathering along both sides of the main drag, some setting up chairs on the tree lawns. They rise and applaud as the honor guard goes by. There are smiles and cheers as each float passes. Kids beam as they peddle by on decorated bicycles. Every year a giant truck from the County Road Commission lumbers up the street. It has a huge snowplow on the front and there is always a broken-off mailbox in its blade. The marching band (oh, yes, there's a marching band) is made up of volunteers whose only requirement is to have played once upon a time in high school or college. The Leland band has one rehearsal a year and that takes place an hour before the parade.

For many, the best part is always toward the front. There, right behind the fire trucks is Uncle Sam. He's a slender, elderly man of average height with a white beard and mustache, wearing red and white striped pants, a red vest, blue coat, and a red, white and blue top hat. He carries a cane and there's a spring in his step. He's eighty-six-year-old Ted Lanham. He's been playing the role for the better part of fifteen years.

I wanted to meet and talk to Ted Lanham so I visited his farm near Cedar. It's just the kind of picturesque place where you might expect Uncle Sam to live. There's a massive, aged Michigan barn sitting on a fieldstone foundation. The house is very old, but you can tell it's been remodeled with great care. It's covered with brown cedar shakes.

Ted and his wife Tali have known each other since the first grade. They've been married for sixty-two years and have one son.

They grew up in Indiana. From boyhood on, Ted realized he was gifted with his hands. He could make stuff and fix things.

He graduated from high school in 1943 and, with World War II in progress, he immediately joined the Army Air Corps. He flew thirty missions over Europe as a top turret gunner on a B-17. On his last mission over Germany, his plane was so badly damaged by flak that the crew couldn't make it back to England. What's more, the bomb bay doors were stuck open. So Ted, the guy who could fix things, was assigned to the emergency. Straddling the yawning gap, and wearing no parachute, Ted successfully hand-cranked the doors closed.

With France safely in Allied hands, the pilot found a small air-field and landed. The crew left Ted with the plane and headed into a nearby village hoping to find some fun. Ted turned his attention to several abandoned airplanes on the side of the strip, scavenged parts and repaired the disabled B-17. The crew returned, having had a fine time, and hoping to stay for more. They were most disap-pointed to learn they could fly safely home immediately.

Following the war, Ted attended Purdue University, receiving a degree in electrical engineering. He and Tali married in 1950. What followed for Ted was a highly successful career owning a distribution business for GE products. He retired in 1981 and the Lanhams moved to their Michigan farm.

Ted continues to use his hands. He fly fishes. He builds and re-stores wooden canoes. He makes and pilots radio-controlled soar-ing gliders. His property displays another of Ted's talents: pieces of metal sculpture that he creates from scrapped farm machinery. There is a tall, thin bird which he has named "Jeanne Crain" Then, there's the gaunt figure of a man, which Ted has dubbed "Iron Will." A smaller piece is "Buster Crab" and another is a metal dog that seems to have been out in the elements for some time. Ted calls him, "Rusty."

He's happy in his retirement, but what seems to give him the most pleasure is his annual role as Uncle Sam. Because he marches near the head of the procession, he's finished early and wends his way back through the crowd as the parade continues. Parents often ask, "Can we take a picture of you with our kids" and Ted complies with a smile. He usually asks the children, "Do you know how old I am?" He seldom gets the answer he wants which (this year) is "two hundred thirty-six." That's because he considers Uncle Sam's birthday to be 1776.

I went home, did a bit of research and called him. "Ted," I said, "The character of Uncle Sam didn't emerge until 1813. You're only one hundred ninety-nine years old!" "Oh, I know that," he replied. "It's just that '1776' has a much better ring to it. Besides, I chose long ago to never become confused by the facts."

Ted Lanham, my kind of Uncle Sam. ⋏

Fred Atkinson – Revisited

August 2009

The very first of these tales that I brought to you was about Fred Atkinson. I chose him because he literally lived next door to me in Leland. I'm going to tell you his story again, but this is not a rerun. It's an update. I think you'll understand when I'm finished.

I'd known Fred for a number of years as a neighbor, and become aware that he'd had a distinguished career as a school superintendent in Minnesota and Michigan. On a summer afternoon, I'd often see Fred, a tall, lean man, puttering around in his yard and whistling softly to himself. Like as not, his wife June would be inside preparing supper. The delicious aromas that came from her kitchen and wafted across the lawn made Fred smile with anticipation.

One day, I was attracted to an emblem on his license plate I'd not noticed before. It read "Ex POW." I asked him about it and discovered a dramatic chapter in his life.

Fred told me that in the spring of 1941, he was finishing up his third year at Lawrence College in Appleton, Wisconsin. Those were tense times in our nation and Fred was certain he was going to be drafted, so he took the bull by the horns, boarded a bus to Milwaukee, and enlisted in the Army Air Corps. He was in flight training when Pearl Harbor was bombed. America needed pilots fast and so in October of 1942, less than a year from his first solo flight, Fred found himself flying a B-25 headed for North Africa.

His squadron was assigned the task of bombing ships in the Mediterranean carrying fuel and supplies to General Rommel's tank corps. On his first mission, Fred flew in the wing position beside General Jimmy Doolittle. That mission was successful.

The crew on his plane was composed of Fred and four others. On his second mission, a photographer from *LIFE* magazine rode along to document the war from the air. The date was February 22, 1943. Out over the Mediterranean once more they spotted a large enemy vessel. As Fred moved in on it, two Messershmitts descended from the clouds and moved in on him. The enemy ship opened up with heavy guns and Fred's crew released their bombs scoring direct hits. Fred was flying at two hundred seventy-five miles an hour a few feet above the water, when his left engine gave out. Whether it was the ship's guns, the fighters', or just bad luck, Fred would never know. The left wing of his B-25 caught the water and the plane cart-wheeled into the sea.

Fred's co-pilot, John Hartley, was thrown free. Fred was strapped to his seat in the sinking plane but somehow fought his way to the surface. He saw Hartley and the plane's life raft, which had luckily ejected and inflated. The two men reached it and pulled themselves aboard. Just then, the two German fighters dove from the sky toward the helpless airmen who expected the worst. The planes, however, did not open fire. They simply waggled their wings and headed for the horizon.

It was then that Fred and his co-pilot realized that the other three crewmembers and the photographer from LIFE had perished.

Within an hour an Italian ship approached and a rope ladder was lowered. John Hartley struggled up to safety. Fred grabbed the ladder but realized something was wrong. He was in pain and couldn't climb. The Italians signaled for him to hold on and they pulled him aboard. On deck, Fred passed out. Two-and-a-half years later he would learn that he had broken six ribs and his collarbone, but for the present, he would have to mend without medical attention.

Fred and John were now officially prisoners of war. They were interred in camps in Italy and then Germany. After two years of incarceration, while in a prison camp not far from Berlin, Fred and John could hear distant artillery and knew the Russians were closing in. A blizzard was raging and temperatures dropped below zero. German officials suddenly announced to the ten thousand prisoners that they should gather their gear and prepare to leave. The forced march lasted for three brutally cold days. Fred estimated that around two thousand of his comrades died on that march.

In February of 1945, Fred and John found themselves in a camp with some fifty thousand other prisoners of many nationalities. There was little food and much suffering. Finally, in early spring, forces under the command of General George Patton liberated them.

In June of 1945, the two men, still together, arrived in New York City. Each headed home; Fred to Milwaukee, John to Fenton, Michigan. After a joyous homecoming, Fred drove east to visit his co-pilot and meet his family. There he was introduced to John's sister, June. It was love at first sight.

So now, let's jump ahead to the present. For several years Fred had been suffering from ill health, a "bum ticker" as they used to say. A couple of weeks ago, Fred, now eighty-nine, seated in his favorite chair, passed away holding June's hand. You see, from a tragic plane crash there emerged a great love story. Fred and June had been married for sixty-four years, and he died holding the hand of his co-pilot's sister.

Of course, death and birth are parts of life, but I cannot help but note that we are losing our heroes.

Fred Atkinson ... a hero, a neighbor, my friend. ⚜

Foodies

Give fools their gold,
and knaves their power;
Let fortune's bubbles rise and fall;
Who sows a field or trains a flower,
or plants a tree
is more than all.

John Greenleaf Whittier

A good farmer is nothing more or less
than a handyman with a sense of humus.

E. B. White

A bottle of wine contains more philosophy
than all the books in the world.

Louis Pasteur

Whenever I was called a gourmet,
I suspected I was being accused of
something slightly unpleasant. But that
was before I heard the term "foodie."
I am still not sure that gourmet
is a good thing to be, but it
must be better than a foodie.

Mark Kurlansky

Think of the wonders of uncorked wine!

Horace

John and Phyllis Kilcherman

NOVEMBER 2009

It was a stunning early-October day. The trees were just starting to turn. The sky was a deep shade of blue. There were puffy white clouds. It felt like being in a scene from a Walt Disney movie. I was driving on a country road a mile or so north of the village of Northport. There, at an intersection, I saw a rustic sign. It read, "CHRISTMAS COVE FARM. ANTIQUE APPLES. CIDER." What is an antique apple? The image of some dried up seventy-five-year-old piece of fruit popped into my head. I had to take a look.

I coasted into the farmyard. The house was on the left. Whirligigs spun in the yard. On the right was a large barn, doors wide open, revealing lots and lots of apples. People were milling about, checking out the varieties. When I entered, my eye caught the sight of empty bottles, myriads of them on shelves, floor to ceiling on every wall. I met Phyllis Kilcherman, the lady of the farm. "What's with all the bottles?" I asked. "Oh, that's my husband, John," she sighed. "He collects things. Years ago, pop bottles drew his fancy. He thought there might be fifty varieties. He got into it and now has more than ten thousand. All one-of-a-kind. We know he's got more than the guy who holds the Guinness record. John wanted to put up shelves in the house for them, but I said, 'No way!' So, that's why they're in the barn."

Phyllis invited me into the home — a lovely, warm, cluttered farmstead where you can sense that great meals have been cooked and fabulous pies have been baked. I was immediately struck by three fully-decorated Christmas trees in the living room! And it was early October! "Oh," Phyllis explained, "we never take them down. The oldest has been up for fifteen years now. We just think that we need them at a place called Christmas Cove Farm. I tell you, sometimes when we settle in here on a July evening and light the trees, we can stop traffic half-a-mile away."

Her husband John came in to join us. He had the look of a farmer, overalls and ball cap. He and Phyllis are round, jolly folks, both in their late seventies. "What's an antique apple?" I asked. John told me they are the old varieties that have not been messed with genetically and have been disappearing from orchards for years. They are the kinds of apples our ancestors ate and loved. "I just wanted to save them," he told me. So years ago he bought old books and journals about apples, some long out-of-print. He also sought knowledge from nurserymen and began to gather seeds and saplings. "Today we have around two hundred forty varieties here," he told me with pride.

As a boy, John grew up on a farm less than a mile from his current place. He'd pass his future home riding on the school bus and dream of owning it some day. Farming was just in his blood. He and Phyllis met at a high school dance in Traverse City. He was the country bumpkin, she the city slicker. She laughingly remembers it as "hate at first sight." But over time, things changed for the better and they married in 1952. At first, Phyllis worked as a licensed practical nurse, but with the arrival of three children, she needed to be at home. For twenty-one years John worked as a maintenance man at the Northport School.

With help from John's parents, they were able to buy their farm in 1955. At the time it was bleak and deserted. The old saltbox house was run down and the paint was chipping off, but it would become home. John started planting apple trees. He knew how long they take to mature, so he also planted strawberries for a quicker cash crop. John's job at the school supported them. Everyone in the family worked the farm. "It's a very demanding life," Phyllis says. "Our kids grew up knowing how to work."

Today the farm thrives. Their retail operation buzzes on autumn afternoons. Sometimes as many as a thousand people a day visit them. They are drawn there to sample the apples and watch the cider mill in action. At times, four generations of Kilchermans are serving the public from the barn.

"Folks come to taste the past," John says. They can eat an apple that grew in the time of Christ. They have Thomas Jefferson's favorite apple, and one of the varieties planted by Johnny Appleseed. They sell the old-fashioned Snow Apple that our ancestors carried in their school lunch buckets. Phyllis' favorite is a variety called Ingrid Marie which was first grown on the Isle of Flynn off the coast of Denmark.

"Everybody has an apple story," says John. "They were married under an apple tree or had a swing in one. An old guy came in here recently, bit into a Ben Davis apple, and started to cry. It reminded him of his childhood."

A few years ago, an article about the Kilchermans appeared in the *The New York Times* and was reprinted in other papers as well. Orders for gift boxes flooded in from all over the country and from as far away as British Columbia.

I wanted to know what the future held for Christmas Cove Farm. John said he didn't know. It doesn't appear that the children will want it. They have other interests. Phyllis would like to see it preserved in some way. "There's a lot of history here," she says.

For now, the Kilchermans are happy with their lives. "We do it because we can," Phyllis says with a laugh. "We're both physically and mentally fit." And they certainly appeared that way. I asked them, "Do you eat an apple a day?" John thought about it and said, "No, but during the season we eat all the varieties, mostly to see if they're ripe."

So there you have it. Because I turned off the road and followed the sign, I discovered several things. I learned what an antique apple is, and I met two wonderful, happy people who love being around apples … and maybe that's enough to keep the doctor away. ⚘

Bernie Rink

MARCH 2009

A friend, who regularly listens to this program, told me, "You've got to meet Bernie Rink. You can find him at the vineyard. He's there every day from 1:00 to 5:00."

I discovered his place was not easy to find. I drove south from the village of Lake Leelanau down a county road, up a hill on a smaller winding country road, and then onto a lane that threaded through a stand of evergreens. And there it was. The building looked like a cross between a chalet and a warehouse, not the usual "winery chic."

The interior conveys that same feeling. Paintings, photographs and newspaper articles randomly cover the walls. There are several unmatched chairs. The bar rests on six varnished barrels, and a fire crackles in the open woodstove that provides the heat. If you're used to the toney tasting rooms found at the newer vineyards, that's not what you'll find at the Boskydel Winery. Yet, there is a great deal of comfort, especially on a frigid late-winter afternoon.

Bernie Rink is eighty-two. He's a large man with thick graying hair and heavy glasses. He wore lace-up boots, a checkered shirt, and wool trousers held up by wide suspenders. All in all, his attire gave him the look of a rather well-dressed old lumberjack.

He grew up on a truck farm in northern Ohio near Lake Erie. Bernie says, "The farm was nothing but work but because of it we lived well for the time." The "time," of course, was the Depression. He says they always had enough to eat: milk, butter, fruit, vegetables, meat, and there were grapes. His father had a vineyard. It was big enough that each fall they could store twenty barrels of wine in a cellar under the kitchen. Not a bad supply to have, especially during Prohibition.

Bernie went to Cleveland for his higher education, earning a Master's Degree in Library Sciences. He took a job with an extension of the Michigan State Library driving a bookmobile around the state. That's how he found Traverse City and Northwestern Michigan College. He got a job there cataloguing books and soon was made the school's first librarian, a position he held for thirty years. He bought a home in the country. It came with some acreage, providing lots of space for him, his wife Suzanne, and their five sons. It was there that Bernie and the boys fashioned a baseball diamond. It became quite a popular neighborhood spot.

He had many interests including Inuit art. He bought and sold pieces for decades. Any money he made from the art sales, he used to buy pieces for the college collection, which you can view now on permanent display at the Dennos Museum. It is one of the world's most important collections of Inuit art.

One day back in the early '60s, Bernie was driving through Leelanau County admiring the orchards. Thinking back to his childhood, an idea popped into his mind: "I don't get it," he thought. "All this fruit up here but no grapes. Why not?" As a librarian, he had access to a wide variety of books so he began to read about wine-making.

The boys knew something was up when he plowed the ball diamond. He started slowly in 1965 buying thirty-five varieties of grapes and planting ten vines of each to see which would work. Five years later, he planted the vineyard on sixteen acres. In 1975, he built the winery. The name "Boskydel" was inspired from writings of an old English professor whom Bernie remembered and admired. "Boskydel" roughly means "shady wood or valley."

The boys were put to work in the vineyard. Bernie says, "Well, they might have been chasing all over the county getting into who knows what. I turned those five potential 'liabilities' into five 'assets.'"

As for the sons, they grumbled some. They chopped weeds during the heat of the summer, picked grapes in sometimes "iffy" autumn weather, and pruned vines in the chill of winter. But they found ways to turn their work into fun, even making up songs like:

We work at Boskydel,
The closest thing to hell.
We're never treated well,
At slave camp Boskydel.

Yet, Bernie was onto something. The answer to his question regarding the lack of vineyards in the area was simply because no one had done it. Today there are nearly sixty wineries in this part of Michigan and Bernie was there at the beginning. Oh, it's true that by the time Bernie opened, some others had started making wine up here, but his was the first estate-bottled winery in the region.

His sons have all grown into well-educated, happy, family men. All of them now agree that their "Boskydel Basic Training Days" added much to their lives, including a strong work ethic. A couple of years ago Bernie's wife of more than a half a century passed away. He asked the boys if he should get rid of the winery. They said, "No. We want to keep it in the family."

And so for now, you can find Bernie every afternoon in the tasting room sitting next to the wood stove. "You know," he told me, "I keep the prices of my wine down so people can afford to put it on the table, not just for holidays." Then he added, "This place only started turning a profit fifteen years ago. I've never taken a salary from it."

"Why do you do it then?" I asked.

"I enjoy it," he replied. "Besides, doing nothing is very tedious. You've got no reason to sit down and rest."

You know, I'm glad I took my friend's advice. Meeting with Bernie Rink by a woodstove on a winter afternoon was indeed time well spent. ⚘

Bill Fraser

APRIL 2010

The name of the place is "Jesperson's," a café in the heart of downtown Petoskey. It's been there for one hundred seven years. I heard it might be a good story, and if I wanted a really fine piece of pie, that was the place to go. I called ahead, talked to one of the owners, Bill Fraser, and made an appointment for two o'clock on a given afternoon. But just for the heck of it, I arrived unannounced two hours early so I could check out the place on my own.

The first thing I noticed was that Jesperson's looked like a scene from a Norman Rockwell painting. There was a lunch counter with fourteen stools. There were also lots of simple tables and chairs. It was bright, friendly and, above all, wonderfully old-fashioned.

I spotted a guy I was pretty sure was Bill Fraser, a large, bald man with a flowing white mustache and a twinkle in his eye. He had the look of somebody's favorite uncle. He was seated at a table near the kitchen wearing an apron.

I checked out the menu. One word stuck out: "homemade." There were homemade soups, homemade breads, homemade rice pudding, and, of course, the menu proudly mentioned "Jesperson's award-winning homemade pies."

I first ordered a Reuben sandwich. It was just fine. Then I cast my eye toward a wide shelf behind the counter that held the pies. I whispered softly, "Get thee behind me, Satan" … but it did no good. When I saw among the offerings "Banana Cream Pie," I was a goner. I couldn't remember the last piece of banana cream pie I'd had. It was like eating ambrosia with a cloud on top.

I departed from Jesperson's a happy man and wandered about Petoskey until two o'clock. When I returned I discovered that Bill Fraser was indeed the guy at the back table. "You were just in here!" he said with surprise. "Yes," I replied trying to sound mysterious. "Sometimes I work undercover." "Well," he said. "I could tell you were a stranger. I know just about everyone who comes in here and can call most by name."

I learned that Bill had grown up downstate and moved to Petoskey in 1967. He was working as a salesman for a fly-fishing company. He met a young woman named Bobbe, and they soon became an item. Her dad was the second generation of Jespersons to own the restaurant and she would become the third.

Bill knew nothing about the restaurant business but found himself increasingly involved. He learned on the job. When Bobbe's father was getting ready to retire, the question arose as to who was going to make the pies. Bill volunteered but that made Bobbe nervous. A Jesperson had always made the pies! "I'll get dad to check you out," she said. So, her father, a man of few words, came in. Bill rolled out a crust for him, filled it, and popped it in the oven. The old man muttered simply, "You got it," and he left. Bill has made all the pies ever since. He estimates he makes eight thousand each summer and in the last twenty-five years he believes he has made more than two hundred thousand pies, all from scratch. He buys his fruit locally and gets the flour directly from a mill.

Bill told me a story about a woman who had called ahead to order a pie to take home. Unfortunately she arrived to pick it up too early in the morning. (They don't open until eleven.) She had a forlorn look on her face so Bill let her come inside to wait. "What's that whirring noise?" she asked. Bill told her it was the mixer whipping egg whites into meringue. "Oh my goodness," she uttered. "I never dreamed! What do you do with the yolks?" "We put those in the fillings," Bill answered. "We don't use that prepared gelatin stuff here." The woman had just learned she was not in a fast-food joint. "That's right," Bill told me. "We make all the soups ourselves. We roast the turkey breasts daily that go into the club sandwiches and chef's salads. We want you to eat food that tastes like your grandmother cooked it in her own home."

That probably explains why there's so much loyalty and history at Jesperson's. Some families have been coming for four generations. As a young man, Ernest Hemingway was a regular. Bobbe's dad remembered him as a silent guy. Tourists sometimes ask Bill where Hemingway sat. No one in the family remembers exactly, but that answer doesn't satisfy folks, so Bill points his finger to one stool or another and announces, "That one. That makes 'em happy," he says with a chuckle.

Bill told me when resorters pay one last visit to Jesperson's before heading home for the fall, they often say, "This is so good. Don't you ever retire!" That made me ask him the obvious question. "Well, Bobbe and I can't go on forever," he replied. They have four children, but none seems anxious to take over. Some of the grand-children show interest but Bill's not sure he can wait that long. "If we were ever to close, there'd be such an outcry," he says, "and a lump in my throat, I can tell you. One hundred seven years! That's a long time."

I looked up from the table and saw five older men wandering in. They wore checkered shirts, overalls, work boots, and baseball caps. "Oh," Bill observed, "Here comes the 'Three O'Clock Group' for coffee." As I was leaving, Bill walked over to talk to two ladies sitting at a table near the front window. Each had a piece of pump-kin pie topped with a puff of fresh whipped cream. I looked back at that old-fashioned room and thought to myself, "You know, I really love slow food." ⚶

John and Julia Brabenec

JUNE 2008

I headed up the Leelanau Peninsula toward the village of Northport. I was looking for the home of John and Julia Brabenec. Their directions brought me to a two-track that led across a meadow to a grove. As I entered the woods I passed a large vegetable garden and a barn. The home was a handsome, modern two-story structure built of wood and fieldstones.

John and Julia came out to greet me. They were small, lithe folks who appeared to be in their late seventies. Both looked like they got plenty of sunshine.

We sat in the cozy living room and their story unfolded. They met in Detroit and a few months after their first date, they were married. That was in 1948, which means this year they'll celebrate their sixtieth anniversary. They both worked at the *Detroit News*, John as a dispatcher, Julia in national advertising. They honeymooned in a cabin on the water in Northport. The rent for their ten-day stay was a staggering thirty-five dollars!

John decided to become a printer, which meant he had to serve an apprenticeship. His salary was miniscule. They had to live on forty dollars a week. This was when they became big-time recyclers. They abided by a motto Julia had heard somewhere: "Fix it up, wear it out, make do." In other words, live frugally.

They planted a garden and after a couple of years John built a small home by hand. He'd never done anything like that before, but it served them nicely. Their first child was born, John became a fully-qualified printer, and their income improved. Nonetheless, they clung to their belief in a simple lifestyle.

For a while, they continued to vacation in Northport but as two more children arrived and as their garden grew larger, they stopped traveling north.

Years passed and they moved to Canada and then Colorado. Along the way, John built five more homes for his family. He got so good at it that he stopped working as a printer and took up the building trade full-time.

When their children grew and left home, the Brabenecs began to think of Leelanau County again and of all the good times they'd once had there. They traveled back, found fifteen lovely forested acres near Northport and bought it. John built what they called a "temporary home." In actuality, it was a barn they planned to use for storage later. They were about a mile from the nearest power line so they decided to live without electricity. They used kerosene lamps, heated with a wood stove, and pumped water by hand. They again wanted to live simply, and that's what they did.

They put in gardens with the idea of growing organic vegetables for themselves and to sell. Soon they bought an adjacent fifteen acres and planted eleven hundred apple and peach trees.

Julia was getting tired of living in the barn, so John began work on yet another house. But the orchard and gardens took time and he could only work on the home sporadically. Labor was especially demanding when the peaches reached the point of perfect ripeness. John and Julia would pick furiously, often until dark. Then, on little sleep, they would drive to farmers markets in Midland and Bay City. Their organic peaches were a rarity in Michigan and sold well.

As time passed, they found some other closer markets including Oryana, the natural foods store in Traverse City.

One day, Julia looked at John and said, "You know, we've been living in our temporary home for almost thirty years now. I think it's time for you to finish the *real* house." So, with help from a daughter and a son-in-law, they did just that, moving in three years ago.

As I sat in their living room, I was struck by how comfortable it was. But here is the kicker. As they did in the barn, John and Julia live completely off the grid! Their electric power is generated by a windmill and solar panels. There is plenty for lights, washer, dryer, radio, and television. They still heat with wood. They do use a small amount of propane to heat water and to cook. No hardship is apparent at all. That's because there isn't any. They live as nicely as you and I.

I've heard it said that living off the grid is not possible here in our neck of the woods. There's not enough sunlight in the winter. Wind is unreliable. But the Brabenecs are living examples of why that perception is not true. They pay no electric bill, no water bill, and no heating bill. And when the power goes out for the rest of us, the Brabenec's lights are always on.

They are happy people. When I asked what had been most important in their lives, John was quick to answer, "Our love for each other."

John and Julia Brabenec, who still recycle and still abide by the motto, "Fix it up, wear it out, make do." ... and live simply but well. ⚘

John and Anne Hoyt

November 2007

John Hoyt has bright eyes, a wide smile and a shock of unruly dark brown hair. He looks to be in his mid-forties. On the morning when we got together, I found him standing in the middle of a bright, tiled room wearing rubber boots and a gauzy white hat that covered that mop of hair. I'll explain his costume in a moment or two.

John grew up around Detroit. He attended Wayne State University, became enamored with the French language, and decided to become a teacher. In 1982, as he approached his junior year, he felt a strong urge to go to France to immerse himself in the language. The only rub was that he had very little money. Yet, off he went and, to make ends meet in France, he got a job picking grapes. He soon discovered that the Swiss paid better wages to their pickers, so he traveled there. He knew that communicating would not be a problem. In that part of Switzerland, folks spoke French.

He found work and lived in a Swiss village. He slowly got to know the locals, among them some cheese-makers who told great stories about their lives high up in the mountains. John became intrigued. In 1985, he enrolled in a nearby school to formally learn about cheese, and on the side, he worked as an apprentice.

The next year, he got his first real job with a small operation, some seven thousand feet up in the Alps. It was a rustic life. The farm had no running water and no electricity, but John adapted and discovered that everything about cheese-making fascinated him, everything, that is, except milking the cows. On this farm, the cows were of a very small breed, with very small udders, and John, who has big hands, found the chore nearly impossible.

Then one day in 1986, a French girl named Anne showed up at the farm while mountain hiking with a girl friend, She was a petite, pretty young thing with a lively sense of humor. John liked what he saw, especially when he learned that she had milked small goats in France. Anne, with some encouragement, decided to stay at the farm for a week and help out. One thing led to another, and Anne and John fell in love. As John now puts it, "She knew how to milk those little cows. How could I let her go?"

They were eager to learn more about cheese-making so the couple began taking jobs at a variety of enterprises in the Alps. They fell in love with a kind of cheese called Raclette.

By 1988, John felt he'd learned enough. It was time to go back home. Anne liked the idea of a move as well. They still had very little money, yet they had a big dream of making cheese in this country. And not just any cheese, but that special Raclette. John was relatively sure almost nobody was making it in the United States.

In Detroit, he quickly finished his academic degree as they explored possible locations to set up shop. Mostly, they looked in Michigan. When they discovered Leelanau County, John was thrilled. It reminded him of the Bordeaux region of France.

They moved north, still broke. Anne got work on an herb farm. John did odd jobs and tried to raise money to begin their cheese business. He could find no investors.

To get started, he needed a hundred-gallon stainless steel kettle at a cost of ten thousand dollars, a hopelessly high amount for John. One day a neighbor, who knew of his plight, asked him to come over. He had bought something at a salvage company that might be of interest. It turned out to be a hundred-gallon stainless steel kettle. John was euphoric! He bought it from the neighbor for one hundred dollars and the promise of a lifetime supply of cheese.

Next, the Hoyts needed to find a location. After some intense research, they found an empty garage for rent in the tiny hamlet of Omena, made a deal, and set about cleaning and painting the place. In the spring of 1995, they prepared their first batch of Raclette. They stuck a sign out in front that read "Leelanau Cheese" and, lo and behold, the public beat a path to their door. The business grew nicely for several years but their supply could not keep up with demand, even though the Hoyts were working seven days a week!

They began to search for a larger space and finally hooked up with Black Star Farms south of Suttons Bay. The management there thought a cheese-making operation would be a nice fit with their winery. A tiled room was constructed next to the tasting area and fitted with wide windows so parents and children could watch cheese being made.

The Hoyts opened at Black Star in September of 2000. Anne was worried. "Now we'll probably have to make more cheese," she moaned. And she was right. Their production tripled and soon they realized, to their joy and dismay, they still couldn't make enough cheese to satisfy the demand for it.

In the meantime, they began entering contests. Their cheese won some impressive awards in Michigan and Wisconsin. In 2006, they entered the American Cheese Society competition in Burlington, Vermont. It's a very prestigious contest that is considered a premiere event in the industry. The Hoyts were thrilled to have their cheese named "First Runner Up." They entered again in 2007, and, believe it or not, their aged Raclette was named "Best of Show." They had beaten some twelve hundred other cheese-makers.

John was ecstatic! He told me, "This is like winning the Stanley Cup in the cheese industry." Anne's response was "Oh No! Now even more people will want our cheese!" And once again she was right. Orders were coming in from all over the country.

The Hoyts live in a warm, inviting farmhouse in a valley south of Lake Leelanau. It's a good place to sort out the problems caused by having too much success.

If some day you find yourself south of Suttons Bay and you happen to drop in at Black Star Farms, peer through the glass window and you'll see John and Anne in their funny white hats and rubber boots making the best cheese in the nation, and you'll know how this story began for the two of them, in a beautiful mountain meadow in Switzerland. ⚘

Jess Piskor and Abra Berens

MAY 2010

Today's subject is about spring, but it begins in the autumn. Yes, last fall a friend of mine said, "You and your wife have got to come with me to the farm and see what my son is up to." "The Farm" turned out to be a lovely spot on the Leelanau Peninsula west of Northport. We turned off the road onto a half-mile dirt lane flanked on each side by rows of ancient cherry trees. Our car entered woods on a bluff that abutted Lake Michigan and then we walked to a hand-built cottage. The westward view over the lake was breathtaking. There we met Jess Piskor and his business partner, Abra Berens. Both are twenty-seven. They were fine looking young people with deep tans and wide, bright smiles.

We had been invited to dinner. Jess and Abra had prepared five courses, starting with devilled eggs and homemade pickles, followed by duck and chicken toasts. The menu included pan-fried summer squash with herbs. There was roast goose and a blueberry geranium sorbet. The finale was a cherry-peach cobbler. I've been to many high-end restaurants that couldn't match what those kids had done. Then came a surprise. We were informed that virtually everything we ate that evening had been raised by Jess and Abra on the adjoining farm!

Their story begins downstate. Both graduated from the University of Michigan and both found jobs at the legendary Zingerman's Deli in Ann Arbor. Jess sold cheese. Abra took orders and worked in the kitchen. That's where they met each other. While they were there, Zingermans opened a restaurant called "The Road House." The chef became unhappy with the produce he was buying so he started raising his own tomatoes. That was the beginning of what became a huge garden. Jess was assigned to work in it. One day as he was harvesting vegetables he had an epiphany. He thought to himself, "This is what I want to do for the rest of my life!"

Meanwhile, Abra was becoming very interested in cooking. She shared those thoughts with Jess. The two of them began to talk endlessly about food. She applied and was accepted at Ireland's premiere cooking school, Ballymaloe. For three months, she trained in the kitchen there and worked on the school's hundred-acre organic farm. Abra returned to this country to Chicago and began working in some of the city's finest restaurants as a line cook and baker. She also dreamt of somehow being involved in a small-scale farm.

Jess had grown up in Suttons Bay. His grandfather, retired Traverse City physician Jack Fiebing, owns land near Northport. Jess approached him about farming it and an agreement was reached. It included being able to live in the rustic cottage. He then called Abra saying, "My family has some land in Leelanau County. Are you interested in going into business?" She was.

They started last spring with a one-acre plot. They planted tomatoes, corn, onions, arugula, carrots, garlic, cucumbers, beans, peas, kale, chard, spinach, potatoes, turnips, parsnips, herbs, and more. All of their plants were grown without the use of pesticides. They also raised ducks and geese. Their chickens brought them a nice supply of eggs.

Jess and Abra sold their produce at farmers markets in Northport, Suttons Bay and Traverse City.

They settled into cottage living. They have running water and electricity and heat with a wood stove. They have no TV and can only receive a couple of radio signals, yet they claim they're never bored. They read a lot and have learned that a farmer's life is early to bed and early to rise.

They named their operation "Bare Knuckle Farm." It seemed to fit because of the hard work involved, and also, since they reside on the little finger of Michigan, the image of a knuckle came naturally to mind.

At the end of the season, they discovered they had actually made money! It was not a giant profit, but not bad. It was enough to split between them and to buy a hoop house for the next season, which would allow them to get plants started earlier in the year.

I asked Jess how he learned to farm. "Well," he replied, "The experience at Zingerman's helped. I also read a ton of books. And, of course, working at it teaches you a lot." Naturally, there were a few bumps along the way. For example, they learned to pen their chickens after coyotes wiped out their first flock.

In the future, they plan to expand the garden, build a root cellar, plant orchards, and raise pigs. I asked them where they saw themselves in five years. "I'd like to be here," Jess answered, "living in Northport, farming and being part of the community. The people are so warm and welcoming." Abra said she wants to open a restaurant using fresh, organic, ingredients mostly from their own farm.

And there you have it … a story for springtime about hard work and dreams. Next time you go to a farmers market look for Jess and Abra. They're the ones with the wide smiles on their faces. ⚘

Pram and Suzanne Acharya

February 2010

I'd like you to meet Pram and Suzanne Acharya of Charlevoix. Both look to be in their late forties. They have four children. Theirs is a story of hope. Literally.

I'll start with Pram. He has a medium build with a touch of gray showing through his dark hair. He's of Indian descent, born and raised mostly in Bombay. As a child he was witness to poverty. Lots of it. But he was lucky. His parents had means. Both were doctors. They expected their children to be well-educated, and they were. Pram grew up loving language and can speak a number of them. His English doesn't have a hint of an accent.

In 1978, he came to the United States to attend Florida Tech University, a school that specialized in engineering. He helped support himself by working in restaurants near the campus. During his senior year he came to a disturbing realization. He really didn't want to spend his life working as an engineer. Pram dropped out of college and bounced around for a while finding work in restaurants, and he began to gain a real interest in food. He entered Oakland Community College, a culinary institution in the Detroit area. In order to hold body and soul together, he worked on the side as a dishwasher, waiter, or any job he could find. Then in 1982, he became manager of the highly-regarded Golden Mushroom in Southfield, Michigan.

That's where he met Suzanne. She was a small, pretty strawberry blond who was waiting tables. Pram learned that she was an accomplished cook who was running a part-time catering business from her home. She came from a long line of "foodies." During the Depression her Italian grandparents owned a take-out restaurant across the street from the Rouge Plant in Detroit. Hers was a family of six children where hard work and good food were the order of the day. "My mother was an amazing cook," she told me.

Suzanne had worked in the kitchens of several fine restaurants with European chefs and had learned much. Soon she and

Pram discovered that not only did they share a love of good food, they had also fallen in love with each other. They married in 1993.

Pram managed the Golden Mushroom for five years, learning every facet of the restaurant business and becoming an expert on wines. One day, he received a call from Pete Peterson, the legendary owner of the world-famous Tapawingo restaurant in Ellsworth, Michigan. Peterson needed a maitre d' for the summer. Pram had been recommended to him by a wine vendor. It seemed like a good opportunity, so he, Suzanne, and their young family went north.

Pram immersed himself in the job and after just two weeks, Peterson offered him a contract. He loved the work, overseeing every aspect of Tapawingo.

As time passed, Pram and Pete noticed something was changing in the culinary business. Gourmet cooking in the home was becoming more and more popular. People were reading fine cookbooks and creating wonderful meals on their own. Pram began to think about creating a business that would cater to that market. The idea appealed to Suzanne as well. Peterson helped them look for a location.

They found it on the northern edge of Charlevoix, a single-story building just off the highway. They leased the back half and opened in 2001 as a specialty food and wine shop. It was where a person could go to buy the ingredients necessary for gourmet home cooking.

The shop progressed nicely for them. So well, in fact, that after some eight years, with financial help from friends, they bought the entire building. It was their intent to keep selling specialty food and wine but also, to finally have their own fifty-seat restaurant. They opened in April of 2009 naming it after a happy-looking cafe Pram had once seen in Bordeaux. It was called "Esperance."

Suzanne runs the kitchen and Pram oversees the dining room. Their customers seem overjoyed. Pram would have it no other way. After all, he says, "Food is an expression of love."

The menu is not huge: half a dozen appetizers, four main courses to choose from, as well as four desserts, all at affordable prices. The wine list is extensive. Some people arrive and say, "What does Sue want to cook for us? Whatever it is, we'll take it." Then they might turn to Pram and do much the same thing in ordering wine. "Bring us something that goes well with our meal." Now, in lots of establishments that could be a very dangerous thing to do. But Pram says, "It's a demonstration of trust. I'll never break that trust. I'd never burn anyone."

The Acharyas have achieved a goal they once only dreamed of. Oh, and about the name of their restaurant, "Esperance." Well, that's a French word. It means "hope." It's funny how things work out sometimes. I'm sure when, as a young man, Pram left Bombay for Florida to become an engineer, he never thought he'd end up owning his dream restaurant in Charlevoix, Michigan. But, then again, as Pram often says, "Everyone needs a little hope." ⚶

Larry Mawby

AUGUST 2010

I'd known him from afar for some time. I was aware that he was a highly-regarded local vintner whose wine has a fine national, even international, reputation, but I wanted to learn more. I traveled to his vineyard in the hills south of Suttons Bay. As I approached, I saw his sign. (Who could miss it?) It was a very large hand, made of corten steel. The hand was holding a big stainless steel wine bottle. On it was the simple wording "L. Mawby." Long, neat rows of vines begin at the sign and stretch toward the horizon as you drive down the lane. An impressive modern windmill is placed near several outbuildings. We met in his well-appointed tasting room.

Larry is a large man with an easy grin. He's just turning sixty. He apparently likes the color gray. His billed cap was a dark shade of it. His T-shirt was a lighter gray, his vest and trousers were darker in tone. He had a closely-trimmed gray beard. Even his glasses were tinted gray. But I was to discover that there's more to Larry Mawby than meets the eye. In fact, he's really a very colorful guy.

He was born near Grand Rapids on a fruit farm. The family summered in the Grand Traverse area and always dreamed of moving there. When Larry was thirteen they did. They bought and leased farmland where they raised apples and cherries.

Larry went to Michigan State University, graduating with a major in English. He returned to work the family farms for a couple of years. During that time, he developed an interest in growing grapes. He read everything he could about viticulture. In 1975, he bought a thirty-two-acre piece of land and began planting vines. Two years later he started making wine. He learned through experience. Larry called his first wine "Picnic Rosé." Next he made a red wine which he creatively dubbed "Red." Then he produced a white, which he predictably named "White." Business was moderate at first, so he continued working on his family's farms to make ends meet. By the early '80's, he discovered that he was able to support himself just making wine.

In 1984, he began creating sparkling wines. Within the next decade he determined they were his best, and he decided to specialize in just those. Soon the reputation of Larry Mawby's sparking wines spread across Michigan and the country. Connoisseurs and just plain folk sought them out.

I looked around his tasting room and saw lovely pictures on the walls. I remarked that I'd never been in a winery, big or small, good or bad, that didn't have awards plastered all over the place! "That's true," he replied, "but those accolades are only for PR. They really don't reflect the quality of the wine. We've won our share of awards, but we keep them out of sight."

I asked about his windmill and he told me he's concerned about our planet. "This is the only home the human race has," he stated. "We are supposed to be stewards of this earth, leaving things better than we found them." With that in mind, he told me he grows his grapes in as benign a way as possible. He also wants to minimize the use of energy at his winery. That's the reason for the windmill. It generates about ten percent of his need and it's a symbol. So is his electric car. He told me that the windmill produces more energy than the vehicle uses. Therefore, in a way, his car is wind-powered.

I learned Larry got a wake-up call some seventeen years ago. He was diagnosed with colon cancer. The outlook was bleak, yet after a half-year of chemotherapy, he recovered with some new insights. "I learned that mortality is very real," he told me. "I'm more observant now. I understood that in life stuff happens. Worrying about that doesn't help. For example, as a farmer, there's no point in stewing over whether it's going to freeze, or if my grapes will be ruined by hail or wind. I've simply learned not to worry about things I can't control."

I asked what he'd like to be doing ten years from now. He answered that he wants to continue making wine for as long as he can. But he'd also like to do some writing: long poems, essays, stories, and maybe a book on viticulture. Perhaps those dreams are a latter day result of his English major at MSU.

I wondered, if he has such a creative literary streak why he named his first wines with the mundane titles of "Red" and "White!" "Oh, I did better at that as time went by," he replied with a sly smile. And indeed he did. He named one of his wines "Sex." He told me the federal government has to approve what goes on a label and, as something of a surprise, they approved that one. He proudly told me that it has become one of his most popular wines. Then he added, "When doesn't sex sell?"

Yes, there's more to Larry Mawby than meets the eye. ⋏

Artists

I shut my eyes in order to see.

Paul Gauguin

To an engineer, good enough means perfect.
With an artist, there's no such thing as perfect.

Alexander Calder

Love of beauty is taste.
The creation of beauty is art.

Ralph Waldo Emerson

Bill Hosner

September 2010

Bill Hosner is an artist. He works exclusively in pastels, making pictures of landscapes, landmarks, and beautiful portraits of women. He has won a variety of awards in this country and abroad.

Bill Hosner is a tall, thin man who mostly dresses in blue jeans and crisp white shirts. He wears rimless glasses. Behind them are bright blue eyes. He'll turn sixty this year.

I met him at his Traverse City studio. It's housed in a one-story former pants factory. The building has been converted into a series of loft-like units. Bill's studio is an extremely neat, simply furnished twelve hundred square foot space. A large skylight illuminates the back half of it. On the walls there is art. Some is his but also there is work of others he admires. Pieces of his furniture were designed and built by Traverse City artisans.

I was surprised to learn that not only does Bill work there but that's where he lives as well. His bed is behind a screen that partially divides the room. He's designed a small kitchen in the rear.

Bill grew up in Detroit and early on showed artistic talent. He got a degree in fine arts from Wayne State University. His father, a survivor of the Great Depression, was unimpressed with the idea of Bill becoming a painter. "Get a real job," he advised.

So, Bill became a commercial illustrator, and did well at it. Much of his work was for Detroit advertising agencies. He also had some national accounts like *Reader's Digest* and the Kennedy Center in New York.

In the '90s computer art became a strong force in the advertising business. Bill adapted to it but grew uneasy about being pulled away from the kind of work he liked. He was making a handsome living but was feeling frustrated. He really wanted to be an artist.

Over the years, Bill occasionally traveled to northern Michigan to do a little painting. He'd stay in hotel rooms and dream of living here full-time.

Five years ago, after a couple of failed marriages, he found himself single. His two sons were grown and no longer financially dependent on him. The timing seemed right. He took the plunge and moved to Petoskey, where he began to paint like a driven man, loving every minute.

Bill found that he wanted to work outdoors. He liked the experience of watching the light move, feeling the wind, seeing nature change, and those images often found their way onto his canvas. For example, one day he was painting a girl hanging clothes on a line. He started at five in the afternoon. As the sun headed for the horizon, he noticed the girl's shadow falling against the laundry. He loved the effect and added it to the painting. Later, when people viewed the work, they invariably commented on the shadow.

While living in Petoskey, Bill often frequented the Roast and Toast Coffee Shop. Young people worked there, but Bill paid little attention to them except to note their numerous piercings, wildly colored hair, and multiple tattoos. Yet, over time he got to know them, all fourteen of them. He discovered they were a hardworking lot, most holding down two and three jobs at a time. Some were married. All wanted to complete a higher education. They had dreams of becoming a nurse, a psychologist, a political scientist. He heard them talk about saving enough money to go to school, a semester at a time! He realized, that despite appearances, these were just people, good people, trying to find their way through life.

Bill was moved by their stories and wanted to help. But how? He was no longer a well-heeled man. Then he was struck by an idea. He would paint portraits of the coffeehouse kids so they could see themselves as he did, perhaps lifting their spirits. Then he wanted to organize an exhibit of the work, selling the portraits and perhaps raising some money for their education.

He approached the Petoskey-Harbor Springs Area Community Foundation and asked if they would handle the funds. The director was interested and said if the exhibit could raise a certain figure, an annual scholarship of $1000 could be established in perpetuity.

Last month, a gala presentation of the paintings was held at the Little Traverse Regional Historical Society in Petoskey. Seventy percent of the goal was reached in a single evening. To raise the rest, Bill has some ideas. Now, since he's moved to Traverse City, he's working on opening another exhibition of those paintings.

Of course, it's great to help others, but I asked Bill about his own financial condition. Was he able to make it as a painter? "Yes," he replied. "I live simply and make the money I need. Life is a joy."

Bill Hosner says he paints 365 days a year. So, the next time you're out driving through the countryside and you observe a tall, thin, gray-haired fellow wearing a white shirt and jeans, working at an easel, it's probably Bill. And just be aware, it's not every day you can see someone who is actually living his dream. ⚘

Jim and Gail Leone

July 2008

The Leones are folks who have been lucky enough to spread joy to lots of other people … and they've been doing it in one way or another for a long time.

They live in the countryside near Cedar. Their trim, white home sits on a hill with views in all directions. From their porch, you can see Sugar Loaf, Timberlee, and a little stretch of shoreline of South Lake Leelanau.

The Leones wear happy expressions and appear to be in the neighborhood of sixty-years-of-age. We sat down to talk around their dining room table, but my eye was immediately drawn toward the living room to a large, beautiful quilt hanging on a wall. Each panel of the quilt displayed a different representation of an ever-green tree. I came to realize the quilt was symbolic for the Leones. You'll understand that too in a few minutes.

Gail and Jim were married in Pontiac, and lived there for some twenty-five years. At first, Jim worked in the auto industry as a master mechanic. Then by chance, he learned that a nearby ice cream store was for sale. The Leones talked it over and decided that would be a happy kind of business to be in, so they bought it. They worked side by side in the place and indeed they did dispense a lot of joy in Pontiac.

Gail took up a hobby, working with stained glass. One day she went into an art store to buy supplies and she saw a lovely vase. In fact, she found it so beautiful that it made her gasp. She wanted to be able to create a thing like that! A little inquiry led her to the Birmingham/Bloomfield Art Association where they gave lessons in glass blowing. She jumped into that with a passion. She learned what she could on her own, and then entered into an apprenticeship with a professional glass blower. In 1992, she opened her first studio.

The Leones had two children. When they had grown, Jim began to think about retirement. They had visited relatives in the

Traverse City area a number of times over the years and liked what they saw and felt. They bought a thirty-seven-acre plot with lots of open space on a hillside. In 1995 they sold the ice cream shop, built a house and moved north. They also constructed a pole barn on their property and installed a kiln for Gail.

She became inspired by the idea of making Christmas ornaments and set to work, turning out wonderful glass spheres. Each one was different. Each one was beautiful. She created a website and also began wholesaling to high-end gift shops around the country. Jim assisted her in the studio and, because of the skills he'd learned earlier as a master mechanic, he designed and made most of the tools she uses.

Each year, the Leones blow glass from early September until the first week of April in order to avoid working with a kiln during the hot months. Glass blowing can be a dangerous profession and I asked Gail if she ever got burned. "No," she replied. "Not once." She thought for a moment and then added. "Oh, last week I did get a burn from our kitchen stove."

In preparation for the coming Christmas season, they have already created four thousand ornaments and a thousand other glass pieces.

I glanced again at the quilt hanging in their living room, the one that I now realized was filled, not with just evergreens, but with Christmas trees. I thought of the all the happiness the Leones have provided for people for so many years, from ice cream to ornaments. I asked Gail if there was any one principle that helped guide her. She answered, "You know, we have been fortunate, and now that we live in the country and have time to reflect, I purposely try to find one memorable thing to see or do each day. Perhaps it is a patch of trilliums I find in the woods, maybe a maple tree in autumn that glows golden in the light, perhaps a beautiful sunset. Maybe it's sitting down and sending a postcard to a favorite nephew. Or, calling an ill family member just to let them know they're not forgotten. One thing a day ... every day."

Jim and Gail Leone, people who count their blessings a day at a time … and who live with the symbols and the spirit of Christmas all year long. ⚜

Fred Petroskey

MAY 2008

He is not a tall man but he exhibits an imposing presence. His hair is pure white, his bushy eyebrows are black, and his goatee, again is white. He dresses mostly in those colors – black and white. When you observe him attired in black trousers, black turtleneck, and black jacket with a white silk scarf thrown over his shoulders you might say to yourself, "By golly, that guy looks like an artist." And if you'd said that to yourself, you'd be right.

At seventy-five, Fred Petroskey can't think of a time when he was not an artist. His early memories are of living with his family in a former schoolhouse, just outside the village of Lake Leelanau. Blackboards were still attached to the walls, and young Fred could find abandoned pieces of chalk behind the radiators and use them to draw. There were six boys in his family, so there wasn't a lot of extra money for art supplies. When his parents returned from shopping, Fred would collect the grocery bags and carefully cut them to form large pieces of paper to use for his drawing. As a child, he practiced and practiced. "How does a leg look from this angle?" he'd wonder. "Where is the light coming from, and how does it affect the look of this piece of fruit?" He wrestled with per-spective. All of his attempts and successes were achieved without any formal training.

The family moved into the village and Fred attended St. Mary School. He discovered he was much in demand when the nuns needed artwork for posters. After graduating from high school, he did some traveling in Europe.

When he returned to Lake Leelanau, the nuns nudged him into directing the senior class play at St. Mary School. The lead actress was a girl named Molly, and she and Fred soon took a shine to each other. Next came a tour in the Air Force, marriage to Molly, and a degree from Western Michigan University. Molly and Fred got jobs in a downstate regional school where Fred was asked to create an art department. It was satisfying work, and the Petroskeys stayed five years and had three children.

In the late 60's, there was a shortage of educators in our nation, so teachers were in the fortunate position of being able to find work easily. Fred took that as an opportunity to look for someplace new and different to live. At that time, friends from the Boston area invited them for a visit. The Petroskeys were enchanted by it, and decided to move there. Molly obtained a teaching job in an elementary school, and Fred was hired to teach art in a high school in the same system. He also gave private lessons, and taught night classes to adults at the prestigious DeCordova Museum.

Fred started drawing portraits using pastels. At first he did it as a lark, but then took it more seriously, drawing likenesses of his students. At first, he gave his work away, but then parents began to commission him. Early on Fred charged ten dollars for a portrait. Then twenty dollars. The more he raised his prices, the more he sold. The thought occurred to him that maybe he should become a portrait painter full-time.

At age fifty, Fred took early retirement from the school system. With the children now grown and on their own, it dawned on the Petroskeys that they were again free to live anywhere. They scouted around the country. The mountains of North Carolina were enticing, but on a visit back to Lake Leelanau they looked at each other and said "What's wrong with this?" Fred did have a few second thoughts saying to himself, "If I settle here, I'm afraid I'll remember why I left."

But the doubts faded. They bought a rundown 1890's farmhouse just north of town and set about fixing it up. Fred converted an old shed into an airy studio adjacent to the kitchen. He went to work painting portraits, some commissioned, some just for the creative kick.

About twenty years ago, Fred's work was being shown in a Leland gallery. On the night of the opening, he noticed a large ruddy man looking intently at one of his portraits. Fred moved next to him, and the man said, "Gosh, this guy can really paint!"

Fred proudly introduced himself as the artist. He learned that the man's name was Ginty Kastys. They were to become fast friends.

Time passed and Fred continued creating his art. He estimates today that he has completed some two thousand portraits.

About five years ago, his friend Ginty suggested that a book should be made of his work. The idea appealed to Fred. With Ginty at the helm, they set about the task. It was published last fall in a limited edition of one thousand books. And if I may be so bold as to act as critic, I want to say that it is a stunning work. In it are one hundred twenty-five portraits: a flamboyant Suttons Bay attorney looking like a southern planter; everyone's favorite barfly, caught in a rare serious moment, looking utterly noble; an old fellow in a baggy sweater seated on a wooden stool with a broad smile on his face as he plays the concertina; the neighboring strawberry farmer, big, brawny, grinning in a shower of color; the beautiful blond, in a black cocktail dress, pearls at her throat, sitting on a wooden porch swing in her bare feet. There's the portrait of his deceased mother-in-law, with her sweet smile and mischievous eyes. Many think that work is his masterpiece. Some of the portraits are formal, some casual, some whimsical, each with a story to tell. Fred says, "When I paint, I want to make a piece of art. I want it to last."

News of the book spread. The Dennos Museum was approached about doing a major exhibition of Fred's work. They agreed, and in January of this year the retrospective opened. The show was such a hit that it was extended, lasting three months in all.

It has been a big year for Fred. I asked him if he had any regrets about pursuing a lifelong career in art instead of doing something that might have been more lucrative. "I was warned," he answered. "My parents couldn't see how I could make a living drawing and painting, but it's something I just had to do. I have thought about it a lot. If I had millions of dollars, I know I'd sit in my mansion and paint."

Fred Petroskey, a guy who not only looks like an artist, but is one. ⚹

Guido Goldkuhle

MARCH 2008

Sometimes a person's life travels in a circle, and sometimes that's okay.

His name is Guido Goldkuhle. That's an unusual last name, "Goldkuhle." The same for the first name, "Guido." I asked him if he were Italian. "Nope. My family is from Germany," he answered. "I had a great grandfather who loved Italy. So that's how I got my first name."

I sought Guido out because I'd heard he was a wonderful artist, a maker of leaded glass. I discovered he lives with his wife and three young children in a lovely home on the Old Mission Peninsula.

Guido is forty-two. His manner of dress is simple. You could mistake him for a farmer or a carpenter. His demeanor is serious but pleasant.

We entered his home by way of his two-car garage which he has transformed into a studio. As we walked through the house I noticed a beautiful leaded glass window composed of different sized circles. The colors were delicate and in a way the window reminded me of the patterns I've seen in Petoskey stones. I passed the front hall and discovered stunning panels on both sides of the door containing gray and blue leaded glass.

In his living room, we sat in front of a picture window overlooking a dense Michigan forest. No improving on that!

I learned that Guido's parents immigrated to the States in the early 60's. His father was a stained glass artist. In fact, in the family's history there is a long line of marble and glass craftsmen. Guido's family ended up living in northern Virginia because his father got a position working on the National Cathedral in Washington D.C. He created several of the windows there, including the famous Rose Window. His father then received a commission to restore the stained glass in the chapel at Duke University.

Guido's dad had a studio at home, where he liked to work. Often the son would sit in that room watching, listening, glad to be close to him.

For several summers Guido assisted his father on the Duke project, but he had no aspirations of working with glass as an occupation. That was all right with his dad. What he wanted most of all was for Guido to gain a good education. He felt that was the way to get the tools to make a career decision.

Guido did earn a college degree and followed it with an MBA. He found employment in Detroit in marketing. There he met and married his wife Becky. He was fairly successful in his career but he wasn't happy. He discovered he disliked sales and travel. On Monday mornings, he dreaded going to work. He sought professional help from a career counselor. She listened to his story, gave him a test and told him, "You should go to work for your dad."

He followed her advice, moving back to northern Virginia, completing one of life's circles. For the next few years he joined his father. When his dad would look at a piece that Guido had completed, and say, "That's good," it made Guido feel wonderful.

Over time, he came to know that leaded glass would indeed be his future, however, he did not want to specialize in ecclesiastical windows as his father had done. It was time to branch out. Because his wife's family lived in Michigan, Guido decided to look for a location for his business there. He did some exploring, found the Traverse City area, and settled on Old Mission.

He set up two websites, Kuhl Studios and Kuhl Doors. In the five years he's been here in the North Country his business has prospered. He figures he serves forty to fifty clients a year. Last month he sent shipments to California, Texas, Arizona, and Colorado.

He is still in close touch with his dad. They discuss projects, techniques and family matters. Their closeness is partially due to those hours when, as a child, he sat in his father's studio. A bond was created that is strong to this day.

That's one of the reasons Goldkuhle likes working in his own home studio. That way he's sure to see his kids every day. Recently, his six-year-old son was seated on a stool watching him. "You know, daddy," he said, "someday I want to work like you, but not with glass. I want to write and draw." Guido replied that he was going to make certain that all three of his children would get good college educations. "Then you'll have the tools to make good decisions and I'll not worry about you at all." It was advice he'd heard somewhere before.

You know, there's something very powerful about a child sitting near a parent in a studio, watching as objects of beauty are created. And yes, sometimes life's paths lead us in circles ... and sometimes that can be just fine. ⚶

Bob James

July 2007

You may well have heard of the person I'm going to tell you about today. His name is Bob James, and I think there are some details in his story that will surprise you.

Bob was born and grew up in a small town in Missouri. He took up the piano at the age of four. His first teacher was a strict nun whom Bob still admires.

He enrolled at the University of Michigan, attracted by its excellent school of music. He was determined to become a jazz musician but upon getting on campus, was disappointed to learn that at Michigan they taught almost no jazz. Bob settled in, hoping to obtain a good musical education anyway. He did, and eventually earned a Masters Degree. There, at the U. of M., he met a girl named Judy who would become his wife, and still is forty-four years later. As a student, Bob didn't abandon his appetite for jazz. He began playing with professional groups around Ann Arbor and Detroit.

Bob was a member of a student group that entered a jazz contest at Notre Dame, which they won. A judge at the contest was Quincy Jones, who was especially impressed with Bob's artistry. Jones sought him out and a friendship was born.

From Michigan, Bob and Judy headed for New York City. Judy taught school to hold body and soul together, and for two years he looked for work, with little success.

Then his life changed dramatically. He got a call out of the blue from Sarah Vaughn. She had phoned Quincy Jones looking for a piano player, and he recommended Bob. They met. They talked. He played. She hired him to lead her trio and to become her arranger and musical director. It was a job that lasted four-and-a-half years, taking him all over the country and the world.

Bob left her to become the staff arranger for CTI Records, the biggest jazz label in America. They also signed him to his first solo contract and he began turning out albums of his own work. About five years later he switched to Columbia Records to head their jazz department.

In 1978, he got a call from one of the producers of a new TV series scheduled to premiere in the coming fall. The producers were fans of Bob and thought he might be the right guy to come up with a theme for the new show. He composed eight pieces for them. They chose a number he'd entitled "Angela." You know it as the theme for the television series "Taxi." Bob put that composition into a new album that proved to be his most successful solo project to date. It went gold.

Two years later another album went from gold to platinum, and won him the first of his two Grammys.

Bob and Judy had reason to visit Traverse City. Judy's sister lived there, plus the James' daughter was attending summer camp at a place called Interlochen. They fell in love with the area, and in 1983 they bought property on an inland lake near Traverse to use as a second home.

Bob continued to compose, record, tour and play at jazz festivals. And he made a discovery. He was tired of living in New York! He built a recording studio behind his Michigan house and he and Judy settled in. It was a home base from which he continued to travel the world. A favorite destination was Japan. In 2003, on a trip there he found himself looking for a new project. He mentioned this to a Japanese entrepreneur with whom he had become acquainted. The entrepreneur told Bob he was interested in Chinese music and knew some very talented, young Chinese musicians. He added that he could use some help molding them into something special. Bob wasn't terribly interested. He knew next to nothing about China. But the entrepreneur urged Bob to go to the Shanghai Conservatory of Music to hear the kids play and, reluctantly, he agreed.

Once at the school, five musicians, all in their twenties, came in to play for Bob. Each was a soloist. They used traditional, ancient Chinese instruments: a two-string violin, something similar to a lute, another which appeared to be a cross between a harp and a zither, and different sized bamboo flutes. Bob was immediately taken with their sounds. He could speak no Chinese, but somehow he assembled the five soloists together in one room. The musicians were very shy and showed no aptitude for English, so Bob simply sat down at the piano to see what might happen.

Would they catch on? Could they play together as an ensemble? Could they improvise?

He quickly discovered they could. He smiled. They smiled.

Bob recorded the music they made that day in Shanghai and returned to Traverse City to listen to the tape and reflect on what he heard. In the months ahead, he returned to Shanghai several times to rehearse with his fledgling group which he named the "Angels of Shanghai."

In 2005, they performed publicly at the Bangkok Jazz Festival before nine thousand people. The next day the *ThaiDay* newspaper, reviewing the festival, wrote: "…there were a few gems that stood out. Legendary pianist Bob James and the Angels of Shanghai band were the showstoppers. The blend of traditional Chinese music and modern jazz wowed the audience."

Over the next year, the group toured in Asia, going to Indonesia, Korea and Japan. They made a CD entitled, not surprisingly, "Angels of Shanghai."

Bob decided he should put together an American tour. He flew the musicians to the U.S. this past April and combined them with a group of some of his favorite jazz musicians. They started out in Traverse City, performing at the Milliken Auditorium to a packed house. Then they took off by chartered bus to Detroit, Cleveland, Pittsburgh, New York City, and Long Island. The tour turned out to be a great success, fueled by the fact that the musicians knew they were creating something new that audiences loved.

Bob told me that as time went by, he learned the young Chinese musicians did have a command of English that varied from player to player. It ranged from "zero" to "a little" to "some." "Did you ever learn Chinese?" I asked him. "Only a few words," he answered. "I can count to six." That seemed odd so I asked him why to six? "Well, there were five of them and one of me. I'd do a head count every time we got on the bus, so I only had to learn how to get to six."

"But how did you communicate over the past three years? All of those concerts, the complexity of the music, the logistics?"

"We got by," he answered, "but mostly we did it just as we did when I first sat down at the piano with them. We communicated with a universal language … the language of music." ⚘

Dave Lint

DECEMBER 2008

Not so long ago, my wife and I were invited to an exhibition held in Building 50 of the old Traverse City State Hospital. It featured a number of quilts, all made by one man, Dave Lint. There, displayed on the walls of a large hall, were about thirty quilts: some with brilliant colors, some subdued, some with abstract designs, others realistic, one even appeared to be in 3-D. They were astonishing.

I've known Dave Lint casually for a number of years. I've also known him as Dr. David Lint, one of Traverse City's most respected physicians. How could a busy doctor find the time to create so many beautiful quilts? I decided to find out.

I arrived at his large log home on a crisp autumn day. It was set on a wooded hillside north of the city. As I walked across the porch, I heard classical violin music. I assumed he was listening to this radio station. I rang the bell. The music stopped. Dave opened the door, and as I walked in, I saw a violin on the study couch.

"Would you like some coffee?" he asked. "You know I roast my own beans." It was the first of many surprises.

Dave Lint is seventy years old. He retired four years ago after forty-four years of practice. He's a strongly built man of average height with lively, bespectacled eyes. He and his wife Mary just celebrated their fiftieth wedding anniversary. They have five children, and as he puts it, "twelve-and-a-half grand children."

He grew up in downstate Hillsdale where his father taught orchestra and band in the high school. When Dave was a youngster, his dad took him to Kalamazoo to an old German artisan and bought him a handmade violin for three hundred fifty dollars, a pretty penny in those days.

For five summers during his childhood, Dave's father came to Interlochen to conduct the All State Orchestra. The family occupied a cottage on Duck Lake. Dave became attached to the area.

Back in Hillsdale, he played concert violin in the school orchestra. He also liked fly-fishing, hunting, and just about anything to do with the out-of-doors. He admired a doctor friend of his father's, an orthopedic surgeon. Dave loved hearing his tales of repairing people's broken this and that, and he began to think of medicine as a career.

He attended the University of Michigan, majoring in pre-med and he played violin in the symphony there. When he entered medical school though, he had no time for that activity. Dave decided to go into orthopedics because he says, "It's a line of medicine where you can fix things. It makes you feel good."

After his residency he was offered a chance to join a practice in Traverse City and he did not hesitate to accept.

What followed was a long, rewarding but strenuous career. He found he was a doctor twenty-four hours a day, answering late night phone calls and attending to victims of all sorts of accidents. He fixed arms, legs, hips, knees, backs, you name it. Although work was difficult and exhausting, somehow he always found time for his family.

As Dave grew older, he began to think of retirement. That worried Mary. What would he do with himself?

Mary had been a quilter for some time. One day he followed her to a quilting shop and saw a pretty one on the wall. He asked her, "Do you think I could do that?" "Probably," she replied. He bought a quilting kit on the spot, she taught him how to use a sewing machine, and he made one. He entered it in a Traverse City quilt show and won the Viewer's Choice Award.

When the day arrived in 2004 for him to retire, he felt more comfortable because he'd have quilting on his agenda. He loved it because he was striving for a different kind of perfection. "If I make a mistake now," he says, "I can start over. That's not how it works in surgery." To date he has created some seventy-five quilts. He has given a few to family and friends but he doesn't sell them. "It's a personal thing," he says.

Dave has resumed fly-fishing, hunting, and camping. He also bikes, skis, and roller blades. "Exercise is the best medicine," he says with a smile. He has also taken up cooking and the reading of texts on mathematics, physics, philosophy, and religion.

Several years ago, Dave and Mary visited her sister who plays violin in the Milwaukee Symphony. A concert there inspired him to get out that beautiful old handmade violin his father had given him. He has relearned his instrument mostly by reading a book, enough so that he can now play with friends in evening musicales in his log house. "I always dreamed of performing live music here in the great room of this home," he says.

Once long ago, a wise man advised me, "Work hard and play hard ... and never confuse the two." Dave Lint, a guy who worked hard, retired well, and doesn't seem confused about anything. ⋏

Lynne Rae Perkins

January 2007

She's a tall, auburn-haired, soft-spoken woman with beautiful electric-blue eyes. From time to time, when she was a little girl in a small town near Pittsburgh, Lynne would wonder what she was going to do when she grew up. At age eighteen, she still hadn't figured it out. She couldn't imagine what job she would perform five days a week for the rest of her life. Her path led her to the study of art at Penn State University. She discovered it was a good fit. Four years later, Lynne graduated with a BA degree. She went on to the University of Wisconsin in Milwaukee and earned a Master's Degree in Fine Arts. While there, she met a guy named Bill Perkins. They began to see each other a bit, but there was no music in the air, at least not at first.

Lynne found work as a graphic designer in Boston. Bill and a friend bought some land in Leelanau County and began to raise Christmas trees. Bill and Lynne met again by chance. That sparked a long-distance romance involving phone calls, letters, and airplanes.

In 1985, when Lynne had been on her Boston job for a year-and-a-half, she had a falling-out with her boss and got fired! What to do? She called Bill and told him the bad news. He replied. "Come to Michigan. You know it's beautiful and we can live in the cabin I built on my land. I think you'll love it." But he warned her that the cabin was a bit rough.

When she arrived at the property in the countryside north of the little village of Cedar, she discovered that the cabin was a bit more than "rough." It was downright primitive! The interior was only sixteen by twenty feet. There was no phone, no electricity, and no water. Furthermore, the cabin was perched on a one hundred foot hilltop. That made hauling things in, like the water, adventuresome.

In addition to selling Christmas trees, Bill was building beautiful rustic furniture made from branches and twigs. Lynne pitched in and helped him with that. They also worked together enlarging the home, and they constructed a barn-like structure to serve as a workshop where Bill could craft his furniture. On the second floor of the barn, they created a studio for Lynne, a place for her to pursue her art.

Bill and Lynne married in 1988. That same year they put in electricity, a phone, and running water — remarkable improvements! Several years later daughter Lucy arrived, followed by son Frank.

Lynne regularly spent time in her studio, where she painted watercolors and made prints. She sold them in local shops and galleries. She began work on a series of illustrations and a coloring book. Little by little, she assembled a sizeable body of work.

One day in 1993, she heard about a conference that was going to be held in Pittsburgh. If you made application and were accepted, you could have your portfolio critiqued by the art director of a publishing company, Greenwillow Books. It was a company that specialized in children's literature. Lynne had always wanted to create illustrations for children's books and thought the conference might be a place where she could make a connection or two. However, she had no examples that seemed appropriate. She thought if she could come across the right fairy tale, she would make illustrations to accompany it, but she couldn't find a fable that appealed to her. So, she just "made up one in her head" about a little girl, and then produced a set of pictures to accompany the unwritten story. She applied to the conference and was accepted.

In Pittsburgh, she met with the art director for Greenwillow Books, who liked Lynne's illustrations. She asked, "Do you write too?" Lynne told her that she had never tried. She considered herself a graphic artist. The art director gave Lynne her card and asked her to try writing a story to go along with her pictures ... and she promised she would read it.

Lynne went home filled with excitement. She sat down at her desk and, to her surprise, wrote the story in a couple of days. She added illustrations and sent it off. The book was entitled *Home*

Lovely. It was about a little girl who moved into a trailer with her single mother. The people at Greenwillow Books liked it very much and agreed to publish it. The book came out in 1995 to very good reviews, but sales of *Home Lovely* were weak.

Lynne wrote and illustrated a second book, *Clouds for Supper,* which was loosely based on the experiences of her own little family. It was published in 1997. Again it was greeted with nice reviews and disappointing sales, yet Lynne kept plugging along. Two more picture books followed, and then she embarked on a children's novel, entitled *All Alone in the Universe.* It was a sweet story and, of course, it contained numerous whimsical Lynne Perkins illustrations. The book was reviewed favorably by a number of journals and publications, and with this novel, sales were brisk.

Lynne discovered she had fallen in love with the characters she had created in *All Alone in the Universe* and decided to write a sequel. That second novel, *Criss Cross,* came out in 2005. Once again, there were glowing reviews. Unbeknownst to Lynne, her publisher entered the book as a candidate for the Newbery Award. That honor is presented by the Children's Division of the American Library Association, and is considered to be the most prestigious award for excellence in children's literature in America. Only one is given annually. More than five thousand children's books are published each year in this country and about five hundred of those are submitted to the Newbery Committee. So winning the award is a monumental achievement.

In the meantime, Lynne had lots to fill her time in northern Michigan. She had a family to care for. She had her writing and illustrating. What's more, she and Bill were building a new home in the village of Suttons Bay. They were doing most of the work themselves, using recycled materials as much as possible.

One day, her mother called from Pittsburgh to say she had just read in the newspaper that Lynne was a finalist for the Newbery Award. It was a complete surprise. She had heard nothing about it. The next day, a Saturday, Lynne's publisher called to confirm the news and to say the announcement of the award winner would be made on Monday. If Lynne had heard nothing by 8:00 AM on Monday, she would know she hadn't won.

The excitement of it all got Lynne's attention. In fact, it began to consume her thoughts. Writing was out of the question. To occupy her mind, she spent the day Sunday doing manual labor. She scraped old paint from reclaimed radiators that would eventually be installed in the Perkins' new home.

The call came at 7:23 on Monday morning. She had won! By early afternoon, she was on a plane to New York. The next morning, she appeared on The Today Show, and that afternoon she was interviewed on NPR. Soon thereafter, *USA Today* and the *Washington Post* wrote big articles about her. In the next few weeks she did over forty interviews! One morning, she talked by phone to fifteen different radio stations!

Her book zoomed in sales. Within two days of the announcement of the award, Lynne's publisher had received orders for eighty thousand books. *Criss Cross* moved to number three on the *New York Times* Children's Best Seller list.

I asked Lynne how all of this success made her feel? She answered, "You know, over the years I have grown to love librarians. For them to select my book is a great honor." Then she added, "I never dreamed I would be a writer. I thought I was an illustrator. For this to happen is overwhelming, and wonderful. For the first time, I am now really making a living!"

What lies ahead for Lynne Rae Perkins? Well, remember I told you she fell in love with the characters she created in *All Alone in the Universe* and therefore they appeared again in *Criss Cross?* Don't be surprised if they show up once more in a third children's novel. Only this time, I've got a feeling the plot will be filled with mystery and suspense, just the kind of stuff kids love.

Lynne Perkins. Hers is a story of being open to possibility … of not being afraid to fail … and of being able to accept great success and high honor with a quiet smile. ⚹

Fighters

Smooth seas do not make skillful sailors.

AFRICAN PROVERB

Strength does not come from physical capacity. It comes from indomitable will.

MAHATMA GANDHI

If you're going through hell, keep going.

WINSTON CHURCHILL

Sandy Blumenfeld

JUNE 2011

Today's narrative goes under the heading, "How to get up when life knocks you down."

Sandy Blumenfeld is a wiry guy, of medium height, with gray hair and a thick gray mustache. He seems to shave whenever the urge hits him … and that appears to be about once a week. Yet, all in all, he wears his sixty-five years very nicely.

Sandy and his wife live in a ranch-style home just north of Traverse City. A road separates them from the bay. They have four dogs and three cats.

Sandy grew up downstate near Bloomfield Hills. His dad taught him to ski at the age of four, and he grew to be quite skilled at it.

At seventeen, Sandy Blumenfeld enrolled at Northwestern Michigan College in Traverse City. The school was one-fifth the size that it is now but it had a very good ski team. That's what drew Sandy north. He joined the team, and in his freshman year they defeated Ferris State, Michigan, Michigan State, and Notre Dame. Although they qualified for the NCAA Tournament, they couldn't participate because NMC had no budget to send them.

Unfortunately, Sandy was a much better skier than student. He also had some behavior problems, like driving a Cushman Eagle motor scooter through the Student Center. The administration, to put it nicely, invited him to leave.

Sandy went to work in local ski shops in the winter and he drove a Coca Cola truck in the summers. That life appealed to him so much he stayed with it for seventeen years.

During his brief stay in college, Sandy had picked up his roommate's guitar and taught himself how to play. As time passed, he got better and better and began appearing at "hootenannies." Soon he was hired for gigs in local taverns.

Sandy also taught himself how to be a stonemason. He worked at it full-time for years. It was physically demanding, but it provided money and artistic satisfaction. Life was pretty good.

Then came the year of 1990. Sandy's mother was killed in an automobile accident. His dad died seven days later. To make matters even worse, Sandy began losing sight in his left eye and he developed blinding headaches. He feared a brain tumor. When a doctor diagnosed him with multiple sclerosis, he was actually relieved! He was informed that his disease would progress but could be slowed with medication. He discovered that he tired more easily and began to lose some coordination. That forced him to give up the physically taxing work of masonry.

Sandy did not abandon skiing but his skills were greatly diminished. The once strong, beautiful skier found he could only negotiate the easier runs, yet he was grateful for that.

He also learned to adapt the skills he had learned as a mason to create things he could handle, smaller projects, like pretty birdhouses adorned with little stones.

Sandy threw himself more into his music, playing and writing songs. He's a member of a band called "Sour Mash" that performs regularly in the area. And three times a week he's an on-air host at WNMC, the college radio station.

"Do you get paid for that?" I asked him.

"No," he answered. "Almost no one gets paid there."

"Why do you do it?"

"Because it's fun, but also I need to make some atonement to Northwestern Michigan College. I was such a problem when I was a student, I want to give something back to the place."

I asked him if living with MS has given him any insights.

"Yes," he answered. "I've been told that my life expectancy may well have been shortened, so I've learned how unimportant some things are and how not to dwell on them."

Then he told me a story about an Olympic medalist skier named Jimmy Heuga. As a young, hot star he was self-centered and arrogant. Sandy got to know Heuga as an older man who, like himself, had contracted multiple sclerosis. "I was in Colorado at a ski benefit for MS," Sandy said. "Jimmy had transformed into a very kind and caring person. I asked him if it made him angry that he'd gotten MS. He told me that, quite to the contrary, he wouldn't change what happened to him. The disease had given him insight into life and made him a far better person." Sandy told me how Heuga's comment impressed him. It sank in. Sadly, Jimmy Heuga died last year.

I asked Sandy about his goals. "I want to go on playing music and writing songs," he replied. "I want to ski as much as I am able. I want to spend what time I have with family and friends. And I want to be as much like Jimmy Huega as I can." ⚜

Martha Baker

SEPTEMBER 2009

A woman I know said, "You've got to talk to Martha Baker. She's got quite a story!" I decided to pursue it.

Martha Baker lives a short distance south of the village of Lake Leelanau in a lovely home on the water. She's a small, pretty woman with an irresistible gleam in her eyes. In a few months she'll turn ninety.

I had known her late husband Dick slightly. I knew that he was vibrant and very successful. I also knew the Bakers were philanthropic. For example, just locally, they gave a tennis court and streetlights to Lake Leelanau as well as a new gymnasium for the St. Mary School there.

"So, what is your story?" I asked. "Oh, I'm very open about it," she replied. And she began.

She and Dick attended Ohio State University where he was a basketball star. In his senior year they eloped. Martha was nineteen.

Dick graduated in 1939 and was hired by the accounting firm of Ernst and Ernst in Cleveland. It was an entry-level job but Dick rose quickly through the ranks. After only eight years, he was transferred to St. Louis to head the office there.

Along the way, the Bakers had four children and settled into a comfortable life in St. Louis. When, after thirteen idyllic years, he was offered the chairmanship of Ernst and Ernst, no one in the family but Dick wanted to return to Cleveland. One daughter openly rebelled, and was finally allowed to finish her high school senior year in St. Louis. To say that Martha was reluctant is putting it mildly. She was very angry.

Up to that point she had been a social drinker. Now, back in Cleveland, she began to drink heavily. Dick could see the change but was at a loss about what to do. One night, Martha came home from a cocktail party barefooted. She had lost her shoes. On another occasion, her doctor called on a different matter and Martha answered the phone noticeably drunk. She was checked into a psychiatric hospital in Connecticut. It was a four-month stay. She was miserable. A doctor told her that she was too angry to beat her problem by herself and strongly suggested Alcoholics Anonymous. She said she'd go, but didn't.

Martha did remain sober for a year and a half, but then began to drink again as a full-blown alcoholic. She'd start early in the day. She hid bottles all over the house. Shoeboxes were a favorite spot. She'd try AA and then relapse. She did it over and over again.

The children recognized what was going on. Her son would confront her saying, "Mother you've been drinking again." She'd deny it, rush to the kitchen, chew on an onion or a piece of lemon, and then blow in his face. "See, I'm sober," she'd say.

In 1971, her mother was scheduled for major surgery in Florida. Martha flew down in a private jet to be of help to her father and support her mother. At the time, she had not had a drink for four months. The operation was successful. That night, there was a small gathering at her parents' apartment. Martha began to secretly lace her iced tea with bourbon. After her father went to bed, she really "tied one on." In the morning she was badly hung over. She went to the airport and called her mother in the hospital saying, "I've got some sort of flu bug. I can't come visit you today. I've got to go back to Cleveland." To make matters worse, it was her mother's birthday and Martha knew it.

Back aboard the private jet the crew, as usual, opened the bar. The smell of the booze made her sick. What's more, she knew she had just lied to her parents. On the plane, she vowed never to take another drink. This time, with the help of AA, she succeeded.

Seven years after she stopped, Martha was named the first woman president of the Council on Alcoholism and Drug Dependency.

Over time, Dick's career soared. He retired as chairman of Ernst and Ernst in 1977. He then served on corporate boards of companies like GE, Hershey Foods and Textron. But in 1993 this brilliant, energetic man was diagnosed with Alzheimer's and began to deteriorate. At times he didn't know who Martha was. One night, as they sat in the living room, he asked the same question over and over. Sad and frustrated, Martha started for the kitchen. She wanted a drink. But in the dining room, she stopped in horror. She thought to herself, "My God, Martha! What are you doing? You'd throw your sobriety away for what?" And she returned to Dick's side.

He died in 2002. Martha has been sober for thirty-eight years now. Nonetheless, she attends AA meetings twice a week, in the fire hall in Lake Leelanau and in a church in Leland. "I'm not tempted to drink anymore," she told me, "and I respect others' anonymity. But I'm very open about my own alcoholism. If I can stand up and tell my story … and if it might help someone, that's important to me. That's why I go."

Then she looked me in the eye and said, "So, that's the story of a drunk. But let me tell you one more thing. I've found great serenity in sobriety."

Martha Baker. My friend was right. Hers is quite a story. ⚶

Keith Burnham

SEPTEMBER 2008

I've known Keith Burnham for a long time. In fact, we traditionally exchange snowballs at the start of each winter. Recently, however, I discovered there was much I didn't know about him.

We sat down to talk outside his home on a hill near Leland overlooking Lake Leelanau. Keith is seventy-five, energetic, has an unbridled sense of humor, and to put it mildly, he is loquacious.

Keith was born in Riverside, Illinois during the Depression. Keith's childhood was not terribly stable. Three months after his birth, his father abandoned the family. His mother married numerous times and moved to California. Keith remained in Riverside living with his grandparents. He attended school there and early on showed talent in art and design.

When Keith was nineteen, he and three buddies drove downstate to go to a dance. They were passing through farm country when, out of the corner of his eye, he saw a name on a mailbox that was identical to his father's. "Sorry," he told he friends, "I've got to pull in." He knocked at the door and a woman answered. "I'm here to see someone who might be my father," Keith announced. A man approached and said to his wife, "Get out of here. I'll take care of this." Just then a little boy ran out of the back door and scrambled up a tree. Keith thought to himself, "I wonder if that's my half-brother." Keith and the man talked and it soon became obvious that indeed they were father and son. Finally, the man asked, "Do you want a job on the farm for the summer?" Keith said he'd think about it, and left. "I never pursued it," Keith told me. "I guess I felt he hadn't cared for me, so I wasn't going to care about him. I just wanted to see what he looked like." Keith never told his mother about the incident.

Riverside is an upscale suburb west of Chicago. But during Keith's early years it was also renowned for being the hometown of some rather notorious gangsters. Keith was going to a night school and on the side he worked designing craps and roulette tables for

The Outfit. (That's the Chicago name for The Mob.) Keith was doing his job efficiently, but one day a higher-up in The Outfit called his mother in California. "Get da kid outta here," he told her. "Dis is a bad environment." His mother hurriedly flew to Chicago and took Keith west. He enrolled in Los Angeles City College, but didn't stay there long. He would later say, "The secret to my success was that I was never inhibited by a formal education."

One day, he read in an L.A. paper that Lockheed Aircraft was looking for designers. He thought to himself, "If I could design a roulette table, then I could do that." He showed up at Lockheed with forty other guys, took an aptitude test, and was hired. That's because, he found out later, he had achieved the highest score on the test in the history of Lockheed! He started as a draftsman and moved quickly up the ladder, but after three years he yearned to go back to Illinois. So he packed his clothes in a cardboard box and climbed on the train. Once in Riverside, he shoved some of his Lockheed drawings under his arm, applied for a design job at International Harvester, and was hired.

He met a girl named Joanne. They dated for one year, one week, and one day, and got married. Joanne's family had a summer place in Leland, and in 1960 the young couple came north for a visit. That was it for Keith. Once he saw northern Michigan, he was captivated.

The Burnhams had four children and were a close family. "I was a good father," Keith told me. "I still am."

He had an illustrious thirty-four-year career designing at International Harvester. In 1988, he retired and moved north permanently. Along the way, Keith had become a skilled amateur photographer. One day, he went out and bought a new digital camera. It cost five hundred dollars! He thought, "I'd better justify that." Since the kids were grown and gone, he decided it would be a good idea to stay in touch with them every day via the Internet with a photograph and a short message. The first day, he took a shot of the lake from his porch. The next day it was Fishtown, then a sunset, a sunrise, a changing leaf, the first snowfall, and so on. The important thing for him was to post a picture every day.

His son John began passing his dad's emails on to friends who enjoyed them. Son Jim had advanced computer skills and talked Keith into creating a website, lelandreport.com. It started slowly: fifty subscribers, then one hundred or so. A reporter for the *Detroit Free Press* picked up the story. The day after it was published, Keith had fifteen hundred new subscribers. Today, there are nearly six thousand. They reside in all fifty states and in thirty foreign countries. One respondent is a brain surgeon in Switzerland. Keith even gets emails from Russians.

The format is simple: a daily photograph, a weather report, a short message about someone's birthday, a story of a one hundred twenty-five-year-old tree that had to be taken down, or an account of last night's storm, and often a message to one of his children. These are followed by responses from subscribers. Of course, all of it is free, even the occasional ads Keith inserts for friends are at no cost.

The Leland Report is not the only way Keith stays in touch with his children. He emails or talks to them every day. I asked him, "Do you think you are such a caring family man because your father abandoned you?" "Perhaps," he said quietly. "Perhaps."

Keith Burnham, a guy whose life might have gone down the wrong road but didn't, and turned out to be just fine. ⚹

Bill Irvine

JANUARY 2010

Bill Irvine and his wife Joan live in a modern single-story condominium near the shores of Lake Cadillac. He's eighty-two, has a slight build, and wears glasses.

Bill grew up in a small town in Ohio. As a kid he loved the out-of-doors. He spent lots of time hunting, fishing, and he was active as a Boy Scout.

In high school, he dated a girl for a while whose mother was a teacher. "I spent more time talking to her than I did with the daughter," Bill told me. Because he loved being outside so much, the teacher encouraged him to think about forestry as a career and she steered him toward Michigan State University. He met his wife Joan there, and graduated in 1951.

Bill first went to work for the Ohio Department of Natural Resources. Then in 1957 he accepted a job with the US Forest Service and was assigned to the massive Ottawa National Forest in Michigan's Upper Peninsula near Ironwood. There he was named Forest Biologist.

As a young man, Bill had felt pain in his legs and one day, he noticed some swelling in his knees. He sought out his family doctor who diagnosed it as arthritis. "What can I do?" Bill asked. The doctor replied, "Don't stop. Actively use your body but don't abuse it." So, that's what he did and tried never to let the arthritis slow him down.

He was one of the very first biologists in the U.P. who worked to save the bald eagle. Once threatened, they are thriving up there today. Bill proudly says that last year there were two hundred thirty-four nests in Lower Michigan as well, and this spring thirty-seven more were found.

Soon after arriving at the Ottawa National Forest, Bill discovered there was a problem with porcupines. There were too many of them. Way too many! He got the idea of introducing to the forest a member of the weasel family called the "fisher". They eat squirrels, chipmunks, rabbits, and they really, really love to eat porcupines. There's a lot of red tape involved to introduce a new species into a national forest. It took Bill nearly two years to persuade his boss. Bill brought in some sixty fishers that had been live-trapped in Minnesota. They flourished and soon cut the porcupine population by about one-third. Fishers are doing well to this day in the U.P.

From time to time, Bill's arthritis would flare up. On one occasion, he set off on snowshoes over a three-foot snow pack to conduct a porcupine census. The temperature rose and the snow began to melt. It was tough slogging. Suddenly his right hip began to hurt. He was miles from his truck. The pain became excruciating. He started back. He had to use his hands to throw his right leg ahead through the wet snow. As nightfall approached, coyotes began to follow him, yipping. He wanted to rest, but knew he didn't dare. It took him from two in the afternoon until nine at night to struggle back to his truck. Surprisingly, the next day the pain was gone.

After eight years in the U.P., Bill was transferred to the Huron and Manistee National Forests. He and Joan moved to Cadillac with their four children. Bill was the naturalist who identified that there was indeed a bear population in that part of Michigan. He worked at translocating wild turkeys. He was also a part of the team that saved the Kirtland's warbler, his proudest achievement.

In 1987, at the age of sixty, Bill retired from the Forest Service. It was then that his arthritis came on with a vengeance. Now he walks painfully using a cane. He can't manage uneven ground so he can no longer hike on his beloved forest paths. He can get out, when weather permits, on his recumbent tricycle and ride the seven miles around Lake Cadillac.

Yet, the reality is, this once vigorous outdoorsman is often confined to his easy chair in the sunroom, watching the squirrels and birds outside his window. Each morning, he casts his gaze toward a nearby tree. There, on an outer limb he has visitors. Yes, they come almost every day, a pair of bald eagles. They bring him great joy and satisfaction … and are proud symbols, I believe, of a better world made possible because of people like Bill Irvine. ♣

Bob Stehouwer

February 2009

Bob and Kay Stehouwer live in a lovely home in northwest Traverse City near the Willow Hill School. They have two grown children.

Bob is sixty-seven. He went to local schools and then on to Michigan State. Kay also grew up in Traverse City and she chose the U of M. They hadn't met each other until mutual friends arranged a date. Something magical happened with Bob and Kay, and they married in 1964. The next year, with degree in hand, he took a job as a Special Agent with the National Security Agency and was stationed at Fort Meade, Maryland. It was a top-secret job filled with intrigue and adventure. Bob loved the work, but the dangers involved weighed on Kay, so after five years Bob reluctantly resigned. They returned to Traverse City in 1969, and he and a brother-in-law took over the family business, E and J Supply, a plumbing and heating company located on Carter Road. At the time, it was a small operation with about a half-dozen employees, and Traverse City was a relatively sleepy burg. That changed rather quickly as more and more people discovered the beauty and opportunity in this part of Michigan. Traverse City jumped to life, and as building spread, E and J Supply grew rapidly as well.

Bob worked hard and life was good. He and Kay were living happily. He loved golf and was accomplished at it. On the course, he met and got to know another Bob — Bob James, the renowned jazz musician. They became close friends and played golf together often.

In March of 1997, he started feeling strange. He had a headache he couldn't shake. Then one day he fainted. He struggled to a dining room chair to regain composure. Kay found him slumped to one side unable to speak. She called 911 and paramedics were there in four minutes. His life was saved, but Bob Stehouwer, age fifty-five, had suffered a serious stroke.

He was hospitalized for a month. His right side was completely paralyzed. It was two weeks before he could speak, and then only with a slur. There was also disquieting news. A doctor told him whatever progress he would make would be confined to the first six months following the stroke. He should hope for no more after that. Bob vowed he was going to beat that "six month prognosis."

At home, his friend of now twenty-five years, Bob James, came for a visit. It was obvious that Bob Stehouwer would never play golf again. "You've got to find something else to do," James said, "maybe something we can do together. How about art?"

"I enjoy art," replied Stehouwer, "but I don't know anything about how to create it."

"Sketch something," James said.

"But my right hand is useless."

"Sketch a nude," said James, handing him a pad and pencil.

With that, Stehouwer took the pencil in his left hand and tried. Both men were amazed. It was pretty good.

For a period of months stretching into years the two Bobs worked together and apart creating art. Bob James sketched and painted. Bob Stehouwer used his computer to create digital art, sometimes splashing amazing colors across the screen, creating complex abstractions, and expressing himself with realistic images as well, like still-life portraits of beautiful flowers.

In the late spring of 2008, The Art Center in Traverse City on Front Street put on a month-long exhibition of their work. The show was entitled, "Two Best Buddies Named Bob." It turned out to be extremely popular. Both men were elated.

It has been well over a decade now since Bob Stehouwer suffered his stroke. Yes, his right arm still hangs by his side. He walks with a decided limp, but he walks. He can dress himself, and can tie his shoes one-handed. His speech is clear and his eyes sparkle. He smiles often, and so does Kay. Together they have been through a lot, and have learned much about life and love along the way.

I asked him about that "six-month prognosis" the doctor had given him. Had it proven to be true?

"In no way," he answered. "I see a physical trainer three times a week. Every day I commit myself to accomplishing a new goal and I almost always achieve it." He paused and then said, "I want to show you something. It may not look like much to you, but it means a lot to me. Just watch." With that, without aid, he raised his once completely paralyzed right arm and placed it on the table. A smile crossed his face and he proudly said, "There is no six-month limit for me. It's been twelve years since my stroke, and every day I get better."

As I drove home, what he said kept reverberating in my head. I decided it's not a bad thought for me and perhaps for you, the idea that every day we too can get better and better in our own way.

Bob Stehouwer, a wonderful example of the strength of the human spirit.

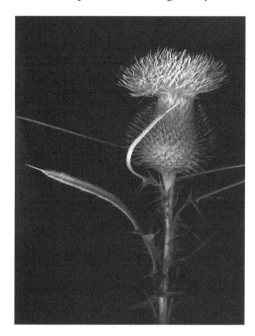

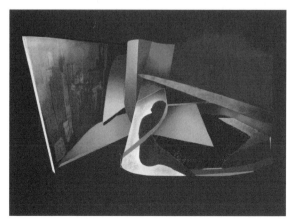

Stefani Pentiuk

October 2011

A listener wrote to me saying that I should meet with a girl in Leland. "Her name is Stefani Pentiuk and she is really something!" I took that advice. Her home is a neat, attractive place, pretty much in the center of the village. Stefani turned out to be an attractive girl with a slight figure and a high piping voice. She's twenty years old and is in her junior year at Hope College.

I learned that her early childhood had been happy and normal. Then in the summer of her eighth year she began to feel unwell. At first, she thought it was just a stomach ache, but it wouldn't go away. There were doctor visits, and trips to the emergency room at Munson Hospital that eventually led her downstate to Beaumont Hospital. There she and her parents learned that a virus had attacked her heart's ventricle system. She was stabilized and returned home.

As weeks passed, the little girl's health declined. A summer resident in Leland, Martha Grogan, heard about her condition. She's a doctor at the Mayo Clinic. After examining Stefani, Dr. Grogan encouraged the Pentiuks to call if their daughter's condition worsened.

Stefani attended her first day of school in the third grade, but became too ill to stay. In fact, she began to turn blue. Dr. Grogan was contacted, and Stefani was flown to the Mayo Clinic by air ambulance. There her parents were given the grim news that Stefani had only a slight chance of survival. They were asked, if a heart became available, could she be given a transplant?

The Pentiuks agreed, and Stefani's name was moved to the top of the transplant list. Three days later, her parents were informed the operation would take place immediately.

One of the cardiologists, Dr. Mike Ackerman, entered her room to comfort little eight-year-old Stefani. "Am I going to die?" she asked him. "No," he answered. "Absolutely not." Then with a smile he added. "In fact, I'm going to dance with you at your Senior Prom."

A twenty-four hour prayer vigil was held at Stefani's church in Leland. That evening a beautiful sunset spread across the sky over Lake Michigan and bathed her hometown with gold and crimson light.

When Stefani was brought out of the operating room, her mother noticed immediately that her cheeks were pink. A three-month recuperation at Mayo followed. As Christmas approached, Stefani was released. When the family drove into Leland, they noticed signs in every shop window and a large banner hanging over the main street reading, "WELCOME HOME STEFANI."

It was good to be back. But Stefani had to take certain precautions. For example, whenever she ventured outside her home she wore a mask. Anti-rejection drugs kept her alive, but her parents were informed that the medications came with certain risks — possible future complications involving other organs.

Slowly, her life returned to normal. Stefani was happy to go back to school and did well. She played baseball and basketball. She swam and even skied.

Twice a year, Stefani returned to Mayo for checkups. When she was a junior in high school, during one of those visits, doctors discovered there were, in fact, complications. Her kidneys were beginning to shut down and she needed to have another transplant — a kidney from a live donor. It was determined that her mother, Heidi, was the best match.

Again the Mayo Clinic came through. Both operations were successful. Stefani's energy returned quickly and her last year in high school was a healthy one. At her Senior Prom, Stefani was dancing with her date when a friend came over to her and whispered, "Turn around." She did, and there, standing in the doorway with a corsage in his hand, was her Mayo cardiologist, Dr. Mike Ackerman. He had kept his promise.

They danced to the song, "God Bless the Broken Road."

As I told you at the beginning, Stefani Pentiuk is now a junior in college. She's studying to become a nurse. It's something she decided she wanted to do when she was eight years old. ⚜

♦

People are hungry for stories. It's part
of our very being. Storytelling is a form
of history, of immortality too. It goes
from one generation to another.

Studs Terkel

Afterword

I want to express my gratitude to all of those who allowed me to tell their stories on the radio and in this work. It has been an honor and a great pleasure to spend time with each and every one of them.

I end each of my broadcasts in the same way, using a kind of signature. I'll conclude this book that way too:

This has been "The Story Next Door." I'm Scott Craig.

I'll see you again, a few miles down the road.

Acknowledgments

I want to thank Thom Paulson, General Manager of Interlochen Public Radio for challenging me to come up with this idea and for including my programs within the schedule of his beautifully managed station. I also want to express my gratitude to IPR producer/engineer Brock Morman for the skill he demonstrates monthly as he puts my stories together for broadcast to the public

I am grateful to the magnificent artist, Angela Saxon, for the design of this book. My thanks also go to John Mitchell for his meticulous critique of my manuscript. I am especiallly indebted to Rose Hollander and her Pleasant City Press for guiding me through the publishing process — and for her patience, wisdom and friendship.

I am beyond fortunate to have two loving daughters, Jennifer Knight and Amy Coleman who, as children, encouraged me to tell them stories, always asking for more. They sometimes lovingly chided me for my occasional urge to embellish upon the truth, a tendency they dubbed, "The Craig Factor." I did my best to heed their advice as I wrote these tales.

Most of all, I want to thank my wife, Carol. I am deeply grateful for her tireless effort, helping to edit the text and photographs contained in these pages. This book was greatly strengthened by her remarkable instincts and insights. Carol is the most accomplished person I have ever known. I am blessed with her talents and love.

Photo: Alden Knight

About the Author

Scott Craig is a retired television producer/director/writer. He began his career in broadcasting in 1957 as a radio disc jockey and two years later broke into television in Champaign, Illinois. He went on to work for the NBC and CBS-owned television stations in Chicago.

In 1975 he formed his own television production company in that city and produced hundreds of documentaries for local and national broadcast venues as well as for the home video market. His programs appeared on CBS, NBC, Turner, Home and Garden, Fox and others. His productions for PBS total more than twenty titles including "Lost in Middle America," narrated by Hal Holbrook; two installments of Frontline; the highly acclaimed, award-winning thirteen-part series, "On the Waterways," hosted by Jason Robards; and the Peabody Award-winning special, "Studebaker: Less Than They Promised."

From 1998 until 2004 Craig produced two series for HGTV: "The Good Life," about people who completely changed their lifestyles; and the popular "Extreme Homes," showcasing some of the world's most unusual domiciles.

Scott Craig and his work have won more than 100 prestigious awards, including a George Foster Peabody Award, a National Emmy and thrity-two Emmys from the Chicago Chapter of the Television Academy. As a result, it is believed that he has won more Emmys than anyone in the history of the Chicago Television Academy. His programs were honored by the Chicago, New York, San Francisco, and Atlanta Film Festivals, as well as the Film Festival of Italy.

Craig holds a BA from the College of Wooster, and an MA and Ph.D. from the University of Illinois. He lives in Leland, Michigan, with his wife, Carol Bawden.